LAMB

BACKWARD THINKING

The Author.

BACKWARD THINKING

BY

JOHN LAMB, O.B.E.

Some Interesting and Amusing Incidents Ashore
and Afloat in the Life of a Marine Engineer.

LONDON

JOHN LAMB PUBLICATIONS AND INVENTIONS LIMITED,
44/45, BILLITER BUILDINGS,
BILLITER STREET, E.C. 3.
1954

Printed by
John Thornton (Printers) Limited
Wallsend,
Northumberland.
1954.

PREFACE

WHEN in the company of friends, generally after lunch at some of the engineering establishments visited in connection with my work, it was frequently suggested that I should write my memoirs. For a long time I did not take the suggestion seriously, then one day, when for some reason I was unable to occupy my time in the customary manner, I amused myself making notes of past experiences, without any intention of continuing.

Some years later I came across these forgotten notes, and circumstances were evidently such that I found myself adding to them, still without any intention of disclosing them to others. As time went on the practice of setting down certain long past but never-to-be-forgotten incidents in my life must have become a sort of mental recreation, since whenever I got a little tired of writing about ships and engines I turned to this new form of relaxation.

The stage was eventually reached when my edited notes were shown to others, who after reading them suggested that they should be made available to those associated with the sea and the building of ships, and that others with a love of the sea would also be interested.

So much has happened in the fifty years reviewed that the difficulty was to select only those incidents which together would give variety, and at the same time keep the book of handy size. I hope readers will find that a good balance has been achieved.

This, then, is how the book came to be written and published, and if it serves to while away a few hours pleasantly and causes an occasional chuckle, I will have no regrets at having taken the advice of my many friends, to whom the book is dedicated.

JOHN LAMB

Monkseaton,
Northumberland.

CONTENTS

CONTENTS

ILLUSTRATIONS

Illustrations by DOUGLAS SMITH

(Cartoonist to Newcastle Evening Chronicle)

FOREWORD

A PIECE of paper for which I paid a shilling at a time when it was necessary to produce proof of my birth, tells me that I first saw the light of day on the 24th August 1890 at a little place called Forest Hall, now a suburb of the city of Newcastle in the County of Northumberland. Although born there, my boyhood was spent in the delightful countryside west of that historic city and within the shadow of Hadrian's famous wall.

My family documented records go back to the year 1700 when William Lamb, who lived in Cheshire, had two sons, John born in 1729 and William born three years later. William, whose direct descendent I am, remained in the north of England, but John journeyed south and official records indicate that he was almost certainly the father of Charles Lamb, the immortal poet and essayist.

William's descendents wrested a modest living from the land in the Counties of Cheshire, Northumberland and Cumberland, and my father and mother were not exceptions. They had two children, my sister Alice dying in infancy. This misfortune was followed soon afterwards by the death of my father, when I was only three years old. It is, therefore, to my mother that I am indebted for my upbringing.

My boyhood was mainly associated with small-scale farming, and I would probably have followed in the footsteps of my ancestors had I not spent some time with my maternal grandmother. She lived all her life in the little village of Ovington, standing high on the north bank of the River Tyne.

Although the chief concern of those in and around Ovington was farming, thriving coal mines on the south bank of the river could be clearly seen from my grandmother's home, as could the beautiful country around the historic Prudhoe Castle when not obscured by the polluted atmosphere.

Grandmother had a good knowledge of the achievements of George Stephenson and his son Robert, and it is not unlikely that what she and, later, my mother, told me about these famous engineers had some influence upon my thoughts for the future. Wylam, the place where George Stephenson was born in 1781, is in the same parish and within walking distance of Ovington, the home of his mother, Mabel Carr, before her marriage.

J.L.

CHAPTER I

FIRST WAGES

I BECAME interested in mechanical things at an early age. Frequently I would walk long distances to see a steam train pass, and stand for hours watching a threshing machine in operation. Nor did my interest weaken as I grew older. On the contrary, as I grew up my interest grew also. With the approach of summer I would eagerly look forward to spending my holidays with an aunt in the mid-Tyne district. When there I could visit the colliery, within easy walking distance, to watch the winding engine at work and lend a hand tipping the coal out of the tubs (four-wheeled bogies) into the railway trucks underneath.

I kept the various parts of the tipping mechanism so well greased that the old man in charge of this particular operation would often say, " Nowt 'll run het while thou's on job." Even in those days I apparently appreciated the advantages to be gained by eliminating frictional resistances, without understanding why. Some years later, when beginning to know something about the theory of lubrication, I remember visiting my old " workmate " and telling him with pride what I knew. He would listen most intently, and his astonishment was evident from his oft repeated ejaculations, such as " Why, mon, dae ye sae see! " and " Noo, w'e'd hev thowt that! "

Whilst waiting some months to begin my engineering apprenticeship, I was sent to work at the Northern Glass Works, known on the foreshore at Gateshead as " the glass house," and, incidentally, received for the first time wages for my labours. This was an exhilarating experience for any boy who had never handled more than the lowest value coins of the realm, and I was no exception.

The " glass house " was mainly concerned with the making of bulbs for electric lamps, and when I recall the methods then adopted, the progress made since the dawn of the present century is really astounding. Those who now tend modern machines which automatically produce scores of lamps every minute, would be astounded no less if they could see the skill and craftsmanship that went into the making of electric lamps by hand in those days.

Picture a low building about 100 feet square on the banks of the river Tyne. On entering the building, which was very sparingly lit by gas jets, it was quite a time before the eyes became accustomed to the dim light. At the far end, however, a narrow beam of brilliant light, like the rays of the sun bursting through heavy cloud, issued from an opening about a foot in diameter in the wall, and round this beam of light could be seen the figures of two men and two boys, the two men moving about in a small prescribed circle with almost mechanical precision and regularity.

As the eyes became accustomed to the light it would be seen that the beam of light came from a crucible containing molten glass, adjoining but external to the building. The heat from this crucible was so great that it became uncomfortably hot at a couple of yards distant, and the light so bright that it was dazzling.

One of the boys was standing and the other sitting. The one sitting might have been me. At first sight he appeared to be sitting on the concrete floor, but upon closer inspection it would be seen that he was sitting upon a piece of wood three or four inches high. Also, that he was bent forward in such a position that his knees were almost on a level with his shoulders and that his hands, which were between his feet, were opening and closing a thing like a pair of giant nut crackers. Actually it was an iron mould weighing about 6 lbs. By his side was an iron bucket filled with water.

The other boy stood beside a hopper-shaped receptacle, alternately receiving from and handing to the men as they passed him what looked like a long steel rod. The men and boys completed a cycle of operations in the matter of thirty seconds, and this went on for twenty-two hours a day, the day being divided into two shifts, the day-shift working from six in the morning until six at night and the night-shift from 6 p.m. to 6 a.m., with two breaks of half-an-hour each for meals. It was necessary for the work to continue more or less without interruption because a vital part of the bulb making in those days was to maintain the molten glass at a fixed temperature, and this could only be done

The one sitting might have been me.

The one sitting might have been me.

with the crude arrangements then provided, by constantly working the crucible.

The only implements used were three iron blow pipes about five feet long, the mould, operated by the boy in a sitting position, an old file, and what looked like a pair of hand shears used by the other boy.

The operation of making a glass bulb began by one of the men inserting one of the steel blow pipes into the mouth of the crucible and rotating it until just the right amount of molten glass became attached to the end. The blow pipe was then withdrawn and the plastic glass on the end rolled on a heated steel slab to give it a circular shape. The pipe was then given a swinging motion to cause the plastic glass to extend endwise, after which the man moved to the mould, which was open ready to receive the end of the blow pipe with the plastic glass attached.

Immediately the blow pipe was in position the mould had to be closed, and the man produced the bulb by blowing down the pipe whilst rotating it between his hands. When the pipe was seen to stop rotating it was the duty of the boy to open the mould quickly and smoothly to avoid breaking the bulb. If owing to drowsiness or thoughtlessness he did not open the mould quickly enough, or jerked it whilst doing so, he received a reminder by having the bulb, then still very hot, brushed against his bare hands.

The blow pipe with the bulb attached was then handed to the boy with the tool resembling hand shears. After nicking the neck of the bulb with the shears the pipe was given a tap, and the bulb fell gently into the receptacle provided for it. He would then clean off the solidified but red hot glass from the end of the blow pipe with the old file, when it was ready for the next man.

This antiquated method of making bulbs for electric lamps may sound very simple. It certainly looked simple, as all operations do when carried out with the skill acquired only by long experience and keen interest. These men were real craftsmen, as will be appreciated when it is mentioned that the crucible contained a measured quantity of material from which a definite number of bulbs had to be produced. Just the right amount of molten glass had to be taken out of the crucible each time a blow pipe was inserted. If more than the correct amount was lifted the expected number of bulbs would not be produced, and a too small amount would result in the finished bulbs being too thin and fragile. The operation was made all the more difficult by the blinding light from the crucible, so that the amount of glass lifted had to be measured by sense of feel rather than sight, and the men generally closed their eyes during this part of the operation.

There wasn't much, perhaps, in the rolling and swinging of the blow pipe, nevertheless the diameter and length of the blob of plastic glass on the end had to be just right when it went into the mould. If not of the correct length the walls of the finished bulb would not be of uniform thickness and its useful life would be short, providing it didn't break during the following stages of manufacture.

To place the blob of plastic glass hanging on the end of a five foot long pipe into the mould located at foot level with the precision necessary was no easy task, while the mould had to be closed by a smooth, swift movement which would obviate the glass touching the comparatively cold mould and thereby cause local chilling. The opening of the mould had to be done just as smoothly and quickly, otherwise the bulb would be broken. After the bulb had been removed there was just time to dip the mould in the bucket of water and have it in position again for the other man, who by that time had dipped, rolled and swung his blow pipe.

The men worked on piece rates, that is to say they were paid so much for a given number of bulbs made, and after paying the mould-holder 7/6 and the other boy 10/- they had about £5 between them for a five day week. Only bulbs that were faultless were paid for, and severe indeed was the reprimand should a boy be the cause of a reject. When compared with present day rates of pay, £2 10s. od. a week doesn't seem very much for such long hours and expert craftsmanship, but the only grumbles I remember were directed toward the boys, whose duties were so monotonous that it was extremely difficult to keep awake on the night shift.

The crucible was recharged at week-ends, it being the duty of the men and boys to mix the sand and soda and add other ingredients, such as red lead, to the crucible, for which they received extra pay. After recharging, the fires were again lighted so that a re-start could be made at 6 a.m. on Monday.

Although glass was first made by the Phoenicians, who I believe taught us to transport merchandise by sea, it was the Romans who realised its value. The legend is that whilst a boat manned by Phoenicians was transporting merchandise along the East coast of Africa it became necessary to beach their little craft to carry out repairs. The cargo of soda had to be put ashore to effect the repairs and for some reason, probably to cook food, a fire was lighted on the sandy beach and some of the blocks of soda were used to enclose the fire. To the surprise of the Phoenicians the soda melted and combining with the sand produced a transparent substance, which we now call glass.

Other materials can be used to allow light to penetrate and at the same time keep out wind and rain, but one wonders what would have been used for electric lamps had that small Phoenician craft not sprung a leak three thousand years ago.

CHAPTER II

LEARNING THE HARD WAY

WHEN barely fifteen years of age I began my apprenticeship at the engineering works of Clarke, Chapman & Co., Ltd., in the industrial town of Gateshead-on-Tyne, my working hours being from 6 a.m. to 5 p.m. Mondays to Fridays and 6 a.m. to noon on Saturdays, for which I was paid 5/- a week.

That my education prior to this was of the most elementary character was proved when I was put to the customary verbal test by one of the factory officials, as I was unable to say my " twelve times " table, sticking on twelve times eleven. However, I was evidently not exceptional, as I was enrolled as an apprentice fitter.

My first impression upon entering the factory and seeing the mass of machinery, both working and under construction, was that in deciding upon an engineering career I had made a great mistake. I felt sure that I could not even learn the names of the machines there, let alone design and construct them.

Everything was so different from what I had expected that I was just bewildered. Not only had I not before seen such compli- cated mechanical contrivances, but the language of the men, and particularly that of the boys, as well as their manners, were completely foreign to me.

My first job at the factory was to fit split pins in the ends of bolts to prevent nuts unscrewing, and in my ignorance I am afraid I wasted much time trying to put split pins into oil holes. Oil holes and split pin holes are often the same size and look alike, but only a greenhorn would expect a split pin hole to be where oil is required. Soon, however, I began to know the difference, and from experiences such as a new factory boy always had to under- go — as, for instance, being sent to the store for a " long stand " and so on — I began to feel that there was a chance that some day I would become an engineer.

During the first year of my apprenticeship I spent my spare

time at various forms of sport, and judging by local junior standards I did pretty well at football and sprinting. Towards the end of that time I began to get interested in the machines building at the factory and felt that I would like to know something of the theory behind them.

My only opportunity to do so was to attend a night school in the town, and I signed on for two nights a week. The session had not proceeded very far before I wanted to study subjects additional to mathematics and machine drawing, but it was not possible to do so at that stage for two reasons, the first being, of course, that it was not permissible to sign up for other subjects in the middle of a session, and, secondly, Mother did not have the money to pay the additional fees nor buy the books required.

To overcome the latter difficulty I hit on the idea of offering my services to a newsagent, and for one shilling and sixpence I collected from the wholesale suppliers in Newcastle, on three mornings each week, two huge bundles of weekly journals and magazines, strung together so that I could carry them over my shoulder. To deliver them to the newsagent's shop in time to allow me to reach the factory by 6 a.m., I had to be out of the house by a quarter to five. Rising so early in the morning and carrying such heavy loads for about half-a-mile before beginning my day's work didn't have Mother's approval, so I had to give it up, but not before I had enrolled as a mechanical engineering student with the International Correspondence School. The fee was £10, which was a very great sum at that time, and the only way I could pay was at the rate of ten shillings a month. I became a keen student and followed their instructions most conscientiously.

This proved to be a wise step, since at the end of the night school session most of the boys stopped studying until the following session, which began in September. As this correspondence course went on all the year round I was able to continue my studies throughout the summer, and not only make up leeway but be well ahead of the other boys when the night school re-opened. The result was that I had less trouble with the work during the session and the examinations at the end.

B

It was about this time that I had to make a hard decision for a boy. As Mother then insisted upon me being in bed by 9.30 p.m. I didn't have sufficient time outside factory hours for both sport and study, and one had to be dropped. Like most boys I was fond of sport, but the desire to know as much as the other apprentices and become a capable engineer prevailed.

I liked the correspondence method of learning, as the little books and instruction papers could be slipped into my pocket and taken into the quiet countryside in the evenings and at week-ends. The only worry was to find the ten shillings instalment at the beginning of each month, so unknown to mother, I bought from the local newspaper depot a number of newspapers on the evenings when I did not go to night school. These were bought for three a penny and sold for one halfpenny each, which to my mind was good business, providing, of course, they could be sold, otherwise it was not so good.

To sell, it was necessary to cover the pre-arranged round quickly and be first there. Although considered a good sprinter, I was not equal to the regular newspaper boys, being handicapped by my boots. I thought of taking off my boots and stockings and carrying them, but realised that I wouldn't be able to run much faster if I had to carry my boots in addition to a bundle of news-papers, particularly as the boots were of the heavy hob-nailed kind bought to withstand the hardest wear. The problem, how-ever, was solved for me in a way worth recording.

The depot where I bought the newspapers was a house, the front door opening on to the pavement in the poorest part of Gateshead. I suppose the occupants of the house received a few shillings a week for allowing their home to be so used. Whatever they got wouldn't compensate, I am sure, for what they had to endure. Imagine twenty to thirty rough, ragged and unruly boys assembling in front of your house an hour before the newspapers were due to arrive, pulling one another about and shouting at the tops of their voices. It must have been Bedlam to those inside.

When the horse-drawn newspaper van arrived it was pande-monium, the boys yelling and making full use of their hands and feet, and sometimes their teeth, to get nearer to the man who was counting and handing out the newspapers. Queuing hadn't been thought of then, so the louder a boy shouted the number of copies wanted and the harder he kicked and pushed, the sooner was he able to start on his round. Often a boy had his newspapers torn before he could force his way through the yelling frantic mob. At first I didn't have the pluck to struggle for my rights, but when on one occasion there were no newspapers left for me I decided to do a bit of shouting, pushing, and kicking if need be, myself.

The woman who lived next door, however, didn't seem to mind the riotous behaviour, because she was always to be found with arms folded and sleeves rolled up to the elbows, leaning against her door frame. Although very stout and obviously poor she had a plump, pleasant face. She rarely spoke to the boys unless it was to rebuke one for striking a smaller boy. It was only then that the smile left her face, but it returned immediately she had given the object of her attention a piece of her mind.

On my second or third visit this good simple soul beckoned me, and when I stood before her she said in the broadest Tyne-side dialect, " How long have you been selling papers ? " I replied " only a short time." She then said " I thought so, because you're not like a paper boy, and, besides, you wouldn't wear those boots if you were. Why don't you take them off so that you can run as fast as the others ? " I told her Mother would be angry if I did, and it wouldn't help much if I had to carry my boots. She then said, " I'll keep them for you until you sell your papers." This she did that night and many nights afterwards. Relieved of this handicap I soon got rid of my two dozen or so newspapers, and when I returned for my boots an hour or so later this good woman always provided a bowl of hot water, in which I removed all trace of having done something which would not have had Mother's approval.

With the few shillings earned in this way I was able, not only to pay off the cost of the Correspondence School course more quickly than was required by the terms of the contract, but to buy a text book now and again from a handcart which took up a position in Newcastle Big Market every Saturday afternoon. These old text books were in various stages of dilapidation and could be purchased for a few coppers. For sixpence one expected the book to be complete with all pages and at least one outer cover. Although it was frequently found that the books purchased had pages missing, it was nevertheless possible to acquire much knowledge from them.

By that time I had become very interested in my studies and there was keen competition amongst a section of the boys at the factory in acquiring theoretical knowledge. From then until the end of my apprenticeship I attended the night school four nights a week during the winter session continuing to study by correspondence during the summer months. My knowledge accumulated and soon I was looked upon as one of the leading apprentices.

In the same category was a boy of my own age named Patterson. He and I became close companions. We attended night school together and then walked home in a round about way in order to discuss at greater length various problems of mutual interest. There was keen competition between Patterson and myself, and generally, but not always, he managed to gain a few more points than I did. As time went on I observed a change in my friend, and although his brain, so far as engineering theory and practice were concerned, remained active and efficient, he became peculiar in other respects, and sad to relate he was eventually put into an asylum where he died soon afterwards.

The district in which I lived during my apprenticeship was called Mount Pleasant. The roads leading up to it are so steep that it was an event to see a horse and cart going either up or down. Even today motor vehicles rarely use the shortest and most direct roads, and when they do they must travel in low gear in either direction. From the top of the Mount one certainly got a wonderful view of the Tyne Valley, but as both sides of the river were then, as now, lined with factories, docks and coal staithes, the view could no longer be called pleasant.

To get from my home to the factory in the shortest time, I had to take one of these steep roads. As it was down hill I could do the journey in ten minutes, but it took quite double that time at my best pace to do the return journey. Being in my 'teens it was

Caught by the foreman making tea.

pleasant enough to journey to and fro for three parts of each year. It was when the steep roads became covered with snow and, worse still, ice, that I wished I lived in some other part of the town.

On such occasions it was difficult to keep proper control of one's feet, and quite impossible during a thaw. The older people made use of a spiked device strapped around the insteps of their boots when the roads were icy, or old socks pulled over their boots when the snow was crisp. The going was so difficult at times that I have seen men climb the Mount on all fours, and women assisted up the hill by a man or boy with a rope tied around their waists as though mountaineering. It goes without saying that we boys had lots of fun when the roads were in this condition, and I am now ashamed to admit that the desire to let the rope slacken quickly, just to see what would happen, wasn't always resisted !

It wasn't so funny when the slippery condition of the roads caused me to go without tea at the 8.30 a.m. break at the factory, especially as tea has always been my favourite drink, and the stronger it is the better I like it. At that time such establishments did not provide canteens, nor even facilities for making tea or heating food. The practice was to take made tea in a tin bottle or can and warm it up when wanted as and where one could. To be caught doing so during working hours by the foreman entailed a reprimand, the severity of which depended upon the mood of that gentleman at the time. My method of overcoming such difficulties was to take a piece of wax candle from home and find a corner not likely to be visited by the foreman, where my can could be hung or stood over the lighted candle ten minutes before the break for the meal, so that my tea would be warm when the buzzer blew.

Mother wouldn't let me use a bottle which could be corked and carried in the jacket pocket because, she said, they couldn't be properly cleaned. I therefore had to take my tea in a can, which had to be carried steadily otherwise much of the tea would be spilled. Imagine, therefore, my futile efforts to reach the bottom of those steep slippery roads at 5.30 a.m. on bitterly cold winter mornings with tea left in the can ! On occasions my legs would shoot skywards and I would land squarely on my back, or other less bony part of my structure, many times before reaching the bottom of the hill. Often have I arrived at the factory with an empty can and had to wash down my cheese sandwich with cold water.

It was about this time that heat-resisting enamels began to be used for pans and other cooking utensils. Mother thought this a wonderful invention as it could be kept clean more easily than cast iron or tin, which always looked dirty even when clean, and when she saw an enamelled can, white inside and bright blue outside, she at once bought it for me.

I couldn't share Mother's enthusiasm for the new can. I felt I would rather be poisoned by the old tin can than be seen carrying that bright blue thing. Some of the apprentices already thought me a sissy, and I knew I would have a rough time when they saw my new can. I was certainly right about that. The can had only travelled about fifty yards inside the factory gates at six o'clock one morning when a boy came up behind me and gave it a kick sufficiently hard to spill half my tea. I ran after him and in the struggle the rest of the tea was lost. During the next few weeks the can was taken away many times without my knowledge, in spite of my efforts to hide it. It would sometimes be filled with greasy bolts and on other occasions oily rags. Finally the boys stood it on the top of a machine and pelted it with bolts and nuts until there was very little enamel left.

I was always a very third-rate pugilist, and although I never intentionally sought a scrap I somehow frequently became involved in quarrels between apprentices. Whether it was my sense of fairness, or just unwarranted interference, I can't tell, but I always took the side which I considered to be in the right and then things just happened. I suppose it was that in spite of past experience I always believed in expressing my opinion to the party whom I thought in the wrong, and his prompt retort would probably be " You keep out of this or I'll punch your nose," and I would probably reply " Two can play at that game," after which a fight would be arranged, generally in the boiler shop during the lunch hour, and invariably I got the promised punch on the nose, which at that time began bleeding at the slightest impact.

A day arrived, however, when I became involved in such a quarrel, and after the combat had been in progress for some time I became conscious that I was at last about to win a fight, much to the surprise of my pals as well as myself. Things were going very well indeed for me in spite of my opponent being taller and heavier, when I suddenly received a heavy blow on the mouth. At first I thought my opponent had kicked me, but it turned out later that his younger brother, who was also an apprentice, had seen, as they all did, which way the fight was going and resolved to prevent his brother losing the day. He was just a little chap who thought better of joining in the fray empty handed and decided to arm himself with a hammer. It was the hammer that hit me in the mouth and broke off several of my front teeth, besides lacerating my lips so badly that it was many days before I could eat food or even drink a cup of almost cold tea.

I had a lot to put up with from the older apprentices during the first couple of years, after which I got a bit tough myself. I was really in an unenviable position during this time because the dozen or so premium apprentices thought me not good enough to associate with them, and the hundred or so ordinary apprentices thought me "too goody" and just the right kind upon whom to play their pranks. After a time my position became more tolerable, firstly because, as I have said, I began to retaliate, and secondly, because I got on so well with my studies. The first had a steadying effect on the ordinary apprentices, while the second gained me the respect of the premium apprentices. In the end I was in the fortunate position of having the friendship of both groups, the only exception being a small proportion of the ordinary apprentices who were bullies and not very nice boys.

Most of the pranks took the form of harmless fun at some boy's expense, such as hiding or spoiling tools and hoaxing. Partly undressing a boy and covering parts of his body with black, red or some other colour paint was indulged in quite frequently. Sometimes, however, the pranking went too far, with serious consequences. For instance, on one occasion a boy threw a smaller boy to the ground and whilst kneeling on him forced the end of a rubber compressed air pipe into his mouth. The bigger boy intended to do no more than that, but one of his friends, thinking he was adding to the fun, turned on the compressed air. The result was that the little boy died in hospital that night.

On another occasion a boy was standing beside a steam engine on the test bed when another boy, thinking to give him a fright, crept up to the engine from the opposite side and opened the steam valve which set the engine in motion. The yells from the first boy made the other shut the valve quickly, but not before the first boy's right hand had been drawn in between gear wheels. This boy, as a result of this stupid prank, had to go through life without a right hand. Many other instances of foolhardy behaviour could be quoted, but these two will suffice to give some idea of the conditions prevailing during my apprenticeship.

The class of work upon which I was engaged during my apprenticeship was not of a very high standard. It comprised the construction of ships' deck machinery, such as winches, windlasses, etc. Assembling would be a more correct description of the work, as the various parts were made on mass production lines, and although the Management did encourage apprentices to attend evening classes and acquire a theoretical knowledge of better class work, learning the trade of fitter was left entirely to the apprentice himself. Fortunately for us boys some of the fitters were expert craftsmen who had previously been engaged on better class work and who were ready to pass on their knowledge.

Assembling ships' deck machinery required a certain amount of skill, and when we boys acquired such skill a transfer to another department of the factory was well nigh impossible, with the result that I began and finished my apprenticeship building winches and the like. The work was paid for by results, the apprentices getting fourteen shillings for each winch assembled, and the men twenty-eight shillings. Many of the apprentices were in consequence more concerned with earning an extra shilling or two than with becoming proficient craftsmen.

A fitter's time rate was then 35/- for a week of 53 hours, and every man and boy had to be working at his respective job five minutes after 6 a.m. or the foremen, who made their rounds at that time, wanted to know the reason why. The first buzzer blew for a few seconds at three minutes to six, and the second and last blew from one minute to six to six o'clock. The factory gates closed immediately the second buzzer stopped blowing, and any who happened to be on the wrong side of the gate at that moment had to return home until 8.30 o'clock and lose quarter of a day's pay. For those who lived too far off to go home and return for 8.30 a public house was conveniently situated near the factory gates, and as it opened its doors at 6 a.m. many apprentices acquired a taste for beer, then three halfpence a gill, through being one minute or less late on a cold winter's morning.

Although hours were long, work hard, wages small, and smoking not permitted during working hours, all seemed happy and contented. Every man's chief concern was to keep his job, and almost every boy's ambition was to secure a berth at sea as a junior engineer at the termination of his apprenticeship. When a fitter wore a peaked cap it was taken as a sign that he had been to sea, and was entitled to and received the utmost respect from all us boys, and invariably that of the men also. How the boys liked to get those old sea dogs to relate their experiences at sea and in foreign ports! Most of the stories of breakdown at sea were doubtless true, if somewhat exaggerated, but we always felt that the stories of nights ashore had to be taken with a pinch of salt.

The wages paid at that time for service at sea in merchant ships were, junior engineers £5, second engineers who had to possess a First Class B.O.T. Certificate £11, and Chief Engineers £18 a month. The pay was not particularly attractive and the living and working conditions enough to put an end for ever to the thought of going to sea, but many boys at that time were prepared to accept, and gladly, such conditions in order to get experience and acquire knowledge of their profession, as well as being imbued with a spirit of adventure which could only be satisfied either by going to sea or joining the army.

Engineers' wages at sea and ashore at that time (1905-10) were very low when judged by present day (1954) standards but the purchasing power of money was very much greater then. For instance, we boys—some of whom probably ate more than the men—could buy at a cafe near the works a basin of vegetable soup followed by as much roast beef and vegetables as we could eat for fivepence, the cheapest cigarettes were five a penny and the most expensive ten for threepence, the best chocolates sixpence a quarter-of-a-pound, work boots 3/6 a pair, boiler suits 2/6, work shirts 1/9, odd trousers 1/6, best suits 20/-, train and tram travel less than a penny a mile, twelve boxes of matches a penny, postage—letters a penny and postcards a halfpenny, footballs 4/6 and football boots 3/6. Mother rented a five-roomed detached house in quite a good quarter of Gateshead, garden back and front, the back containing three greenhouses, for 5/- a week the lot.

Whilst serving my apprenticeship the masters refused a request from the men for one shilling a week increase in the weekly wage, and a strike took place. I cannot remember how long the strike lasted but it was several weeks, and if my memory serves me well, the men got what they wanted before they returned to work. Even then their wage for a fifty-three hour week was only thirty-six shillings, or about twelve shillings a week more than was paid to the unskilled time-workers. The wage of some of the latter, always referred to as labourers, was as low as twenty-two shillings and yet many of them managed to keep a comfortable home and bring up four or five children.

The strike, as far as I remember, was an orderly one. There were certainly no incidents at the factory where I worked. The management naturally made the best use of the apprentices, and in addition to receiving bonuses for greater output, we boys could work overtime whenever inclined. This didn't seem to be resented by the men on strike, so that the boys could be excused for hoping that the strike would not end too soon, as those who didn't wish to spend the extra money in fun and frolic could buy a new text-book or two. Some of the apprentices were sons and brothers of men on strike, a situation which now seems strange and would not be tolerated today.

The chief concern of the men was to get their jobs back when the strike ended. Many of them had been employed at the same factory during the whole of their working life and didn't take kindly to being on strike. The man I worked for when the strike began was so interested in his work that on occasions he would meet me on my way to and from the factory to enquire about the work I was doing, and which he would have been doing but for the strike. If I wasn't doing the work correctly he would tell me how it should be done.

Jobs for fitters and turners were few between 1905 and 1910. There seemed to be two men for every job. At six o'clock in the morning and again at five o'clock at night unemployed craftsmen would wait outside the factory gates for the foremen in the hope of getting employment. There were so many that the foremen just walked along shaking their heads in answer to the frequent requests for work.

I had evidently learned my trade reasonably well, since during the last year or more of my apprenticeship I was allowed to work in the factory from 6 a.m. Friday until noon Saturday, with five breaks for meals, and for the work done during Friday night I received the sum of 1/10d. This may not seem much for an all-night's work, but it did enable me to discontinue the practice of trying to make a few coppers in other directions. During the last year of my apprenticeship I received 12/- a week.

Being at night school on Monday, Tuesday, Wednesday and Thursday evenings, and working all night at the factory on Friday, meant that there was not much time for rest or recreation. My thoughts, however, were not so much of the present as of the future, and I worked so hard at my books that the day arrived when I was asked to enter for the Yarrow Scholarship. This scholarship was open to boys between the ages of seventeen and twenty-one whose parents could not afford to give them a high technical training, and besides the school fees it provided for everything else.

At twenty years of age, however, I was released as a favour from the factory and proceeded to sea, the possibility of gaining the Scholarship being remote. It was not until my ship reached Oran some ten months after leaving home that I received a letter to say that I had won the Scholarship. It was then, of course, too late to take advantage of it, and whilst the disappointment was great,

I resolved that without the higher education I would obtain the degrees which I had stated in my application it would be my endeavour to obtain.

When beginning to get really interested in the trade to which I had been apprenticed, my desire, next probably to that of learning my trade, was to earn a few extra shillings with which to buy technical books. I have already related how I managed to augment my income by selling newspapers and working overtime, but the amount from such sources was rather meagre.

To invent something and sell it to anyone who might be sufficiently interested seemed to be the only way to make big money. Moreover, I could do this, so I thought, without encroaching on my time for study as I could work out my ideas whilst walking between my home and the factory or night school. I was, I suppose, fully aware that much greater minds were wanting to do the same thing but, who could say, I might just happen to stumble upon something that was too obvious for great minds. For instance, had I not read or been told of the crying baby that brought fame and fortune to a very ordinary man who did not claim to have any inventive ability. During one of his daily walks, the story goes, he stopped to find out why the baby was crying and found the cause to be a pin sticking into its little body. The result was the safety pin as we know it today. Then there were, of course, the wonderful achievements of George Stephenson, who couldn't even read or write until he was several years older than I was then.

I had no special line of thought in my inventing. Anything which didn't seem right received my immature attention. For instance, why couldn't railway carriage doors be self-locking so that passengers would not fall out between stations ? Why couldn't sash controlled windows be made rotatable so that both sides of the glass could be cleaned from the inside, instead of women risking their lives by sitting out on the window sill ? Why couldn't a holder for pianoforte music be made in such a way as to obviate the agonising pause between the turning of pages which would not readily separate ?

Many other apparent imperfections in the things which were

necessary to life at that time were given some thought, but like those mentioned, came to nought for reasons which can no doubt be readily imagined.   Moreover, to merely start an idea going required £5, a sum of money that was far beyond my resources. However, whilst I did not at that time receive a penny reward for my earnest endeavours to put things right in the world, there is no doubt that the mental exercise involved stimulated certain properties in me which helped considerably in later years when it was my job to find solutions to difficult engineering problems.

CHAPTER III

IN SEARCH OF A SHIP

WHEN I had completed the fifth year of my apprenticeship there were two obstacles to overcome before I could realise my ambition to go to sea. The first was to obtain permission to terminate my apprenticeship, and the second to find someone who would employ me as a junior engineer on board ship. Both very formidable obstacles in those days.

An apprenticeship of not less than four years was necessary before one could go to sea and, after a period, sit the Board of Trade examinations. I had at that time served five years, so that I was qualified in that respect. I was, however, only twenty years of age and boys had to serve until they were at least twenty-one, no matter when they began their apprenticeship. If the apprenticeship began at fourteen a boy would have to serve seven years, and if it began at seventeen years of age he had to serve until he reached the age of twenty-two.

Apprentices in their sixth year, as I was, were very useful to the factory management because they could generally do a man's job for about one-third the wages. Consequently it was rare indeed for a boy with over five years' training to get release before he had reached the age of twenty-one. Most boys situated as I was endeavoured to get their release by doing as little work as possible and making a general nuisance of themselves. This attitude never seemed to achieve the desired result, so I decided to adopt an opposite attitude. This impressed a junior foreman who had always shown a kindly interest in my progress. As a result he used his influence on my behalf and I got release soon after my twentieth birthday.

I then had to find a job on board ship, and quickly, as my twelve shillings weekly wage was sorely missed at home. Besides writing scores of letters to shipping companies all over the country, I made personal application to almost every shipping company in Newcastle-on-Tyne. Such jobs were so few and the number after them so great that I felt that I had been honoured if my written application brought forth a curt acknowledgement, or my personal application a kindly " Sorry, we have no vacancies." Generally I would climb many flights of stairs to find beside the closed window on which was marked " Enquiries," a notice stating " No sea-going engineers required."

Technical departments of shipping companies always seemed to be at the very top of buildings, and lifts were a rarity in those days. In any case they were not intended for people looking for work. However, I used to console myself with the reflection that nature had provided well for us poor mortals. For instance, it would have been much more trying if the return journey had been up the stairs instead of down ! As it was I, and many on a similar quest, made light of the climb up the stairs because of the hope, even though slight, that there might be a job at the end of the climb.

How I envied Johnny Goodall, whose parents lived near by. Johnny was three years my senior and about this time had been at sea as a junior engineer for two years or so. He must have been on a ship making short voyages for he came home quite frequently. Over a halfpenny plate of hot peas in a little shop in the High Street I would listen with rapt attention to his hair-raising experiences. The ship always made the best speed on Johnny's watch and he never lost the water in the boilers nor let bearings run hot like the other engineers. Actually, Johnny it was who always put matters right and I, at any rate, was quite convinced that the ship would have got along much better without a Chief or Second Engineer.

Johnny was always going to speak to the Superintendent about me. He had only to mention it and I would get a job at once. Whether he ever did pluck up courage to speak or not I don't know, but if he did he evidently did not convince the Superintendent that I was any better than the hundreds of others looking for such a job. I think Johnny must have found it a little difficult to convince the Superintendent about his own ability, because about twenty years later I was told that he was still sailing without a certificate.

I visited ships lying at Newcastle quay on the off chance that a junior engineer would be wanted to replace one who had gone sick or failed to report for duty just before sailing. But nothing came of my efforts in that direction, even though I was prepared to work twenty-four hours a day for any wages offered. It may be that I didn't look the right type for those small hard-case ships, in which living conditions were rougher than anything that can be imagined at the present time.

After a week of fruitless visits to the offices of shipping companies and ships, during which I walked many miles and climbed countless flights of stairs, the chances of getting a job at sea seemed more remote than ever, so I decided to look for employment on shore.

My first enquiry was at a small gear-cutting factory at Gateshead, and by a stroke of good luck an elderly gentleman happened to be passing through the place where callers had to wait, at the moment when I was being told more unkindly than usual by the clerk that they had all the fitters and turners they wanted. The old gentleman paused on his way out and asked me a few leading questions about myself and my engineering experience. He said the only vacancy in the works was for a draughtsman with a knowledge of gear wheel cutting. I told him that although I had never been employed in a works drawing office I had studied gearing at night school, and had picked up a little knowledge of gear cutting whilst serving my apprenticeship. Mr. Martin, the sole proprietor of the small factory, for he it was who had spoken to me, was evidently impressed, for he asked me to go into his private office.

When I knew who it was who had shown kindly interest in me I became nervous and rather tongue-tied. This soft-spoken little old gentleman soon put me at my ease, however, and almost without knowing it I found myself telling him of my burning desire to go to sea. The result of this interview was that I was engaged as a draughtsman at twenty shillings a week, which I considered very generous remuneration as I had no previous drawing-office experience, and had said quite frankly that I would want to leave as soon as I got a job at sea.

During the month or so I was employed by Mr. Martin he taught me a great deal, and when I announced that I had at long last been successful in obtaining a berth at sea he showed the greatest interest and I left with his best wishes. When, however, I was able to fulfil my promise to go and see him upon my return a year later he had passed on. This made me very sad, since although Mr. Martin didn't help me to get what I wanted most, his kindness at our first meeting, his tolerance when I worked for him and his words of encouragement when we parted made a deep impression upon me.

During the forty years which have elapsed since I met this fine old gentleman, I have often thought how important it is to adopt the right attitude towards people, particularly young people beginning their careers. It costs so little in time or effort to show interest and give advice, while generally a helping hand brings its own reward in full measure.

When it was apparent to all that I was determined to go to sea at almost any cost, not, I would mention, in order to see the world so much as to get experience of machinery under service conditions and to qualify for Board of Trade Certificates, Mother took me to a Mr. Bowden, head of an old established business in the city, who was well-known to many Newcastle shipowners. A few days later I was told to hold myself in readiness to join a ship at short notice.

The task of getting my kit together was joyfully started without delay, but this introduced difficulties because Mother could only afford what was absolutely necessary and we didn't quite know what was absolutely necessary. Well-meaning friends who thought they knew, suggested two of everything, so my kit was built up on that basis.

I joined my first ship within two days of being told to hold myself in readiness, and on boarding learnt that I had just sufficient time to slip up the road to a shop where I could buy a straw mattress, known as a donkey's breakfast, for a shilling, together with soap and matches I would require on the voyage. Bedclothes, towels, etc. I had brought with me. Shipowners in those days provided nothing but a seven foot square cabin to sleep in, and even that had in many cases to be shared with another. It was quite common for the second and third engineers to share a cabin, and in some cases the most junior engineer had to share with the mess-room boy. Only the Chief Engineer could be sure of having a cabin to himself.

The conditions under which I would live on board were given scant thought, if any. The knowledge that I had at last got a ship and would soon be keeping a watch in the engine room was sufficient to exclude all such mundane thoughts. How well I remember the thrill of preparing for my first sea voyage, and how proud I felt in my peak cap (without a badge) and my blue serge patrol suit, the jacket of which was single-breasted and buttoned closely around the neck. I wasn't entitled to wear any gold braid, but I had a row of shining brass buttons which more than satisfied me for the time being. I made up my mind that it wouldn't be long before I joined a shipping company which issued cap badges to their officers, and obtained the qualifications necessary to enable me to wear gold braid.

CHAPTER IV

MY FIRST SHIP

IT was on the 6th of January 1911 that I signed-on the s/s *Duffield* as Fourth Engineer. She was in drydock at Wallsend, and on the following day we sailed for Middlesbrough to load a cargo of rails for the Cape to Cairo railway, then in course of construction.

This ship, which carried about 6,000 tons of cargo, had on board only what was absolutely necessary to enable her to get from port to port and discharge the coal, wood or grain cargoes normally carried. Her speed was seven knots when favoured with fine weather and good bunker coal. On one of the few occasions when the Skipper condescended to speak, he told me that the ship had cost £37,000 to build in 1908. I was expected to gasp at the mention of such a vast sum, since the information was volunteered with the sole object of impressing me with the importance of his position as Master. A similar ship would today cost about ten times that sum.

In the engine room the machinery comprised two boilers working at 100 lbs. pressure, a 1200 I.H.P. triple-expansion engine, a stand-by boiler feed water pump, an evaporator, and a bilge and sanitary water pump. There was no refrigerator, not even a dynamo. Fresh provisions lasted two days, after which the staple diet at sea was salt pork, bread and potatoes. The only parts working at sea were the boilers, main engine and the steam steering gear. The evaporator was supposed to produce a ton of distilled water daily but never did, in spite of theories advanced by the seniors and coaxing by the juniors. It nevertheless provided the Third and me with plenty of hard work scaling and making alterations, none of which made the slightest difference to its distilled water producing qualities.

The Chief, Second and Third Engineers all had cabins opening off the tiny mess-room. I, too, had a cabin to myself. Mine, however, was on a lower deck and bounded on three sides by the coal bunker, the hot engine room and the hotter recess containing the noisy old steering engine. On the fourth side was the 'tween deck, into which only hot air from the engine room and coal dust from the bunkers penetrated. My cabin had one small porthole, so that when I wanted to read or write in daytime I had to open the door, or light the oil lamp if I happened to have some of my daily ration of paraffin left over.

During the first few days I didn't notice these deficiencies, or if I did I was much too happy to give them a second thought. All ships were alike to me at that time, and here I was, an officer in one of them. At last I had got what I had so ardently desired for so long. What more could a boy of twenty want?

Having a cabin to myself I felt tremendously important, and on the morning after a night's rest, the first on board a ship, this feeling became more pronounced when at 6.45 a.m. the mess-room boy brought me coffee in a pint pot. After sleeping in a ship's cabin which I had not yet learnt to ventilate, I felt ready for some refreshment and gulped the coffee down. It had not got very far on its journey inside me, however, before a horrible taste of paraffin made me rush to the ship's side and put the coffee, plus what I had taken in the night before, overboard.

We sailed a few hours later for our loading port, and fortunately the sea was calm so all my stomach had to contend with for the rest of the day was the taste of paraffin. I learnt later that the mess-room boy, who was new to the ship, had found a kettle which he presumed was used to boil water. He evidently did not know that some mess-room boys find a kettle a very convenient utensil for filling paraffin oil lamps.

After loading our cargo at Middlesbrough, preparations were made for leaving. Having cleared port, the engines being man-oeuvred by the Second Engineer, our immaculate five feet two Chief Engineer, typically Scotch and almost as broad as he was long, slowly and majestically descended the engine room ladders backwards and, as was his custom whenever the ship left port and the order for " full away " was received, strutted with hands behind his back to the forward end of the engine room. After critically inspecting the water level in the port boiler gauge glass and making sure that the new Junior was observing him, he strutted to the starboard side to inspect the water in that boiler. He then slowly made his way, still with hands behind him and chin well up, to the main engine stop valve.

My station was at the engine room telegraph, regarding the operation of which I had received detailed instructions from the Second Engineer. I was, therefore, able to observe every movement of the great little man without appearing to be too interested. As the Chief approached the stop valve the Second respectfully stood aside and the Chief closed the valve which controlled the speed of the engine. He then slowly and very deliberately began opening the valve five turns, stopping momentarily at each turn as he had done scores of times for the edification of budding seagoing engineers. Having locked the stop valve in that position he came and stood by my side without a word or look. The engines were then revolving at about 52 r.p.m. In my ignorance I thought this a very low speed and that the Chief would soon be opening the valve further in order to increase the speed.

Feeling a little embarassed, as I thought the Chief wished me to express my admiration for the methodical and precise manner in which he cared for the machinery, I could think of nothing better to say than " When do we proceed at full speed, Sir ? " The little man swung round as though shot, and I shall never forget the unreasonably long look of contempt with which he regarded me. No words were spoken, but the effect of that indiscretion was immediately felt and it lasted throughout the twelve months twenty-four days that I served on board that ship. I did my utmost to please during the eleven hours every day I had to work, and if the opinion of others was of any value I did my work well, but it just seemed to be impossible for me to redeem myself in the eyes of the Chief.

The engine room staff comprised four engineers, three firemen, two coal trimmers and a donkeyman. The Second, Third and Fourth engineers and the firemen kept four hour watches, and the trimmers six hour watches. The donkeyman worked from 7 a.m. to 5 p.m. at sea and whenever the cargo winches were being used in port. " Donkey," as he was generally called, had extraordinary

When do we go full speed, Sir ?

"What do we go full speed, Sir?"

endurance qualities. I have known him keep a full head of steam on his coal-fired boiler for a whole week without sleep, or so it seemed. He used to sit on a box when not firing the boiler and the assumption is that he was able to get sufficient refreshment from these odd minutes to keep him going. But never once was he caught asleep whilst on duty.

Being Fourth Engineer I had to keep the 8 to 12 watch. Watch-keeping in a ship's engine room was quite new to me but I had, upon request, been initiated by the Third who had three years' sea experience to his credit. The Second had also given me brief instructions as to the number of drops of lubricating oil that had to be given to each of the various bearings every half hour. What neither of them told me was how to get the drops of precious oil into the bearings that were moving and only came within reach for the merest fraction of a second every revolution of the crank-shaft. This was a part of my job which I had to learn by experience and it wasn't a pleasant prospect, as the Second told me that the quantity of oil he would give me did not allow for a single drop missing its mark.

At last the moment for taking over my first watch came. It was eight o'clock and dark. The thought of being responsible for the satisfactory working of the biggest engine I had ever seen made me feel so proud, so important, but Oh ! so nervous. What if the bearings ran hot because one drop of that half-pound tobacco tin full of oil the Second left me, should miss its mark ? What should I do ? Stop the engine ? No, that would bring down the Chief and that contemptuous, look still fresh in my memory ! Apply extra oil ? No, because there was no extra oil. Whilst searching in my mind for the right answer I looked up, and to my great relief saw Donkey descending the ladders. I didn't know at that time what a heart of gold had this son of Sunderland, otherwise I would have been saved much misgiving.

When Donkey left me about eleven o'clock I knew how to fish oil cans out of crankpits, to repair broken spouts, to feel crankpin bearings without breaking my fingers, to keep the water level in the boilers steady, and, lastly, to make good use of every drop of the Second's precious oil. I learned more in those three hours than in any equal period of time before or since.

During the eleven hours each day, Mondays to Saturdays inclusive, eight were spent on watch and three on maintenance work, which included such items as re-tubing the donkey boiler and fitting a new ash shoot pipe weighing several cwts. through the coal bunkers. On Sundays I had to do eight hours watch-keeping and wash my clothes between the day watches. This gave me little time for study, so when Donkey offered to do my washing for me, I readily accepted. After my morning watch on the follow-ing Sunday, I therefore settled down to my books. I did not get very far, however, before the Chief came to my cabin and de-manded to know what I was doing and why I was not doing my washing. I told him the reason and he at once told me to don my work clothes as there was a job to do. Ever after that I did my own washing on Sundays.

When advising a kit comprising " two of everything " our friends had over-looked the conditions under which junior engineers worked those days. Probably they didn't know that clothes worn in the hot engine and boiler rooms had to be rinsed every day in water limited in quantity and not very fresh. Failure to do so meant that they would quickly rot due to repeated sat-uration with perspiration. Moreover, it was necessary to assist in cleaning boiler fires at the end of each watch, and shoes that had become oily in the engine room, readily burnt when trampling on hot ashes in the boiler room. The result of all this was that by the time we reached Port Said, our first port of call, I was reduced almost to a sarong with a pair of the Third's shoes on my feet. My two new boiler suits went after about a week at sea, much to the amusement of the old Chief Mate who told me that the best way to remove the grease and dirt from them was to leave them for a day in a bucket of hot water to which caustic soda had been added ! I had to learn many things in like manner on that first voyage.

My request to the Skipper for an advance of wages to buy some clothes at Port Said was met with the reminder that I had only half a month's wages (£2 10s. od.) due to me, and that the ship would only be there a few hours anyway. We arrived at our destination — Port Sudan — about a week later and to my dismay I found that if I had been in possession of it, all the money in the world couldn't buy what I so badly needed, as at that time there was nothing there but a native village. However, I didn't feel so conscious of my near nakedness because the natives wore even less. It was not until five weeks later at Calcutta that I was advanced enough money to buy two pairs of drill trousers, six singlets and a pair of shoes, all of which cost less than ten shillings. The Japanese made singlets which could be bought for fourpence each. Ten shillings was the sum advanced, and I remember that I had sufficient change to go up town one evening and buy myself an iced lemonade which, after drinking tepid cloudy water for weeks, seemed the most wonderful drink ever.

By that time I had learned that the *Duffield* was not so comfortable as I had at first thought. The rats came out from the cargo holds and other dark spaces in their hundreds, and after we reached warm climes they were joined by millions of bugs and cockroaches. Sleeping in the bunk was impossible because of the vermin, and after much experience and hard work during the very few hours I could call my own, I found that the only way to get a night's rest was to get a blow lamp and run the flame up and down the tongue and groove boarding. The cockroaches were literally everywhere. If you had happened to look into the mess-room while a meal was in progress you couldn't fail to observe that each time a slice of bread was taken from the plate it was held up to the light and scrutinised before it was eaten. The reason for this was to be sure that a cockroach hadn't been baked in the bread.

After discharging our cargo of rails the ship sailed for Calcutta. We had not proceeded far down the Red Sea when water was reported to be leaking into the centre furnace of the port boiler. After a hurried examination it was decided that one or more of the boiler tubes was leaking, and orders were given for the fire in the centre furnace to be raked out and the fires in the two wing furnaces banked. The Third's suggestion that the two wing fires also might be raked out was not well received. The old Chief refused to shut down the starboard boiler, so that the work of fitting tube stoppers had to be done with the ship under way. To do this, old coir mats, pieces of sacking and tarpaulin were procured and laid along the bottom of the centre furnace. At the time the temperature in the stokehold was something in the order of 120°F., and the temperature inside the centre furnace must have been at least 50° higher.

When all preparations had been made the Second entered the back ends through the furnace and made a hurried inspection of the leakages. Having located and marked the defective tubes the Third was instructed to enter the furnace, and the various tools were thrown in after him. The heat was so intense that it was only possible for the Second, Third and me to work in relays of about three minutes. In addition to the heat, we were greatly troubled by the smoke from the smouldering sacking laid along the bottom of the furnace getting into our eyes and throats.

During my refreshers under the ventilator after a period in the back ends, my thoughts turned to the stories which used to be told to me and my fellow apprentices by the old sea dogs who had served at sea. At the time, we thought that many of their experiences were exaggerated, but this, my first experience of a really tough job at sea inclined me to the belief that the stories they had told were true. My mind went back to one story which at the time seemed very far-fetched, but this particular job made me realise that what I had been told could really happen.

The story was that such a job had to be done on a ship whilst in port. The work was done by shore labour, and during the meal hour the Second Engineer went into the back end of the boiler to see how the work was progressing. He took with him a colza oil lamp which he hung on a projection to free his hands so that he could hammer-test the work which had been done. The vibration caused the lamp to lose its hold, and in his endeavour to catch it, the lamp overturned and the oil ran down his clothing and was, of course, ignited. The induced draught in the back ends caused the man's clothing to burn fiercely, and in his agony he wriggled out of the boiler furnace and rolled himself in a heap of ashes to extinguish the flames. The surprising thing was that this poor man survived, although he was about three years in hospital.

S/S "DUFFIELD" My first ship.

Fortunately nothing of that kind happened when it was my duty to carry out similar work, but under those conditions it can well be understood that it took nearly eight hours to fit two tube stoppers, which in ordinary conditions would have been done in a matter of thirty minutes.

After completing this boiler repair we ploughed our way to Calcutta. Although the weather was reasonably good for the monsoon season, ploughed is the best description. When without cargo the ship was constructed to carry 1,000 tons of ballast water, but the Skipper didn't believe in carrying around too much non-paying freight, so instead of 1,000 tons, never more than 500 tons was put into the ship's tanks. The result was that the *Duffield* rolled and pitched very badly, and the engines raced alarmingly in seas which produced only gentle movements in other ships.

On arrival at Calcutta one afternoon we learnt to our sorrow that we had to make several voyages between that port and Colombo with coal. It was anything but a pleasant prospect, as Indian coal consisted of about fifty per cent. dust so fine that it found its way everywhere, even into bedding and drawers when cabin doors and portholes were shut. Moreover, we knew that the practice was to load and discharge continuously, so there wouldn't be a moment's peace in either port. Our only relief from the stifling heat, coal dust and noise would be at sea, but as the run between the two ports occupied only five days this was poor consolation.

The Chief was evidently well aware of the penetrating qualities of Indian coal dust, because his first order after arrival was to shut the engine room skylights and lock all entrance doors. This meant that the only way that hot air could leave or fresh air enter the machinery space was through the boiler room. The temperature in the engine room rose to 130°F. within an hour, and the Third and I felt quite sure that we would not be asked to do heavy manual work under such conditions. This, however, turned out to be but a fond hope, my first job being to put a turn of packing in the main boiler stop valve glands. The temperature on the boiler tops must have been about 160°F., and tools got so hot that they could only be used if wrapped in pieces of sacking.

Almost before the ship had anchored in the river Hooghli scores of barges laden with coal and many hundreds of brown human beings were making fast alongside. The din was terrific. I had no idea that human voices could make so much noise. What they had to talk about I don't know, but evidently they had plenty. The ease with which the natives got the barges alongside and made them fast to our ship intrigued me so much that it wasn't until I felt a non too gentle tap on the back that I became conscious of the Chief standing behind me.

When I left the engine room some two hours later, loading was in full swing. All four cargo holds were being worked from both sides simultaneously and there must have been a hundred men and women at each. Through the thick cloud of coal dust I could see a gang shovelling the coal with lightning speed into saucer-shaped baskets, each of which held about 20 lbs. of coal. When filled, each basket was at once passed to the human chain extending from each barge to the ship's deck, a vertical distance of about 50 feet at the commencement of the operation. A basket never paused on its journey. They couldn't have been moved with greater regularity and uniformity by a mechanically driven conveyor belt. As the loading progressed the distance the coal had to be lifted became less and the rate of loading increased.

When told that the coal would be loaded by hand I couldn't believe that 6,000 tons could be put into the ship in two days, nor that it was quicker to load by hand than to use the ship's winches. Two days turned out to be rather an exaggeration, but the ship was certainly fully laden sixty hours after arrival. As the last hundred tons or so were being loaded, hatch covers were replaced and other preparations made for sailing, so that almost before the last of the empty barges had cast off the *Duffield* had started the voyage to Colombo. And what a relief to be on the move again with engine room skylights and doors open and the deck hands busy washing down with hoses !

I didn't see much of Calcutta during that first visit to India, but there was plenty going on around the ship. The speed and man-oeuvring qualities, when on the wing, of the swarms of eagle-like birds held my interest, while the bumboat men, snake charmers and fortune tellers provided lots of amusement outside working hours. The birds, being the city's scavengers, were protected by law and were considered so sacred by the natives that any attempt to interfere with their liberty resulted in a stoppage of work. They were so ravenous that all food in the open had to be covered, otherwise they would swoop and grab it in their claws in the twinkling of an eye. On one occasion the mess-room boy was carrying the Sunday joint along the deck and although it was covered by a cloth a bird made a sudden attack. The boy saved the joint but got a lovely pair of black eyes in doing so.

The last cargo of coal loaded at Calcutta went to Djibouti, then a small port at the eastern entrance to the Red Sea. In Colombo we did occasionally get a breeze which made conditions bearable, but in Djibouti the air which was around the ship when we arrived remained there until we left ; it was so stagnant that the fine coal dust rose vertically and descended in the same way on to the decks. So much dust accumulated on the decks that the Skipper made the crew sweep it up and shovel it into the barges, not, I would mention, to make living conditions on board less unpleasant, but to avoid being charged with delivering short cargo. As at Calcutta and Colombo, sleeping was a problem, as apart from the noise, cabin doors and port holes had to be kept closed. The result was that even at midnight the temperature in my cabin was rarely less than 110°F., and with coal dust everywhere, conditions could be likened to living as well as working in a third-rate coal mine. Making oneself clean was impossible, as although the water was reasonably free from coal dust the towels and everything one touched were not.

When at sea it was the practice for the watch-keeping engineers to assist the firemen with the dumping of ashes overboard. With some grades of coal, particularly from Indian sources, it was not unusual to have to manhandle as many as eighty 20-gallon buckets of ashes at the end of each four hour watch in the sweltering heat. I can recall many occasions when for weeks on end the engine room temperature was never less than 120°F., and the stokehold temperature 20 degrees higher.

Warm atmospheres always made me perspire freely and at such times I would work dressed only in a sleeveless singlet of paper thickness, khaki drill trousers and unlaced shoes. Every quarter-of-an-hour or so I would have to remove these garments, wring out the perspiration and empty my shoes in order to be reasonably comfortable. The steel handrails and even the steel tools were much too hot to touch with bare hands, while the drinking water, gallons of which I drank every day, was very often 100°F., even when it was kept in the coolest place on board the ship.

From Djibouti we went to Karachi to load a cargo of grain, and great was our delight when we learned that this cargo was for Bremerhaven, Germany. From Bremerhaven we went to the river Tyne, and arrived there twelve months and twenty-four days after I joined the ship. Looking back at the places I had been to, what I had done and what I had endured, it seemed like as many years. During those twelve months twenty-four days I wasn't given much time for study, but I nevertheless felt qualified to sit the Board of Trade examination for a Second Class Certificate, and decided to leave the ship at the first opportunity.

We arrived in the river Tyne one afternoon about 3 o'clock and moored opposite Pelaw at buoys some hundred yards or so from the South bank of the river. Word went round the ship that we were to be paid off next morning at the Newcastle shipping office. This news pleased me very much, as after getting a close view of the old country I was more desirous than ever to get clear of the *Duffield*. To my surprise the Chief tried to persuade me to make another voyage, saying that the examiners would fail me because I was so young and had served only twenty-four days above the minimum time required.

What a thrill it was to see my homeland again and know that I would soon be seeing my dear ones ! How familiar was everything in sight. Only a few hundred yards further up the river was the gear-cutting works where I had been employed as a draughtsman. It would, I thought, be nice to see Mr. Martin again and tell him about my experiences. He would be very intrested I knew. What surprised me was that nothing seemed to have changed. There was the Newcastle quay as busy as ever. Even some of the ships lying alongside loading and discharging cargo were known to me. On the Newcastle side there were the Cathedral and Castle Keep and on the Gateshead side St. Mary's Church in which my wife Mabel and I began life together, looking, strangely enough I thought, just as they did when I went away. Twelve months twenty-four days is as nothing in the life of such edifices which have withstood the elements for hundreds of years, but I had travelled far and seen so much since I last saw them that I expected them to have changed, if only a little.

After enjoying the fresh air and feasting my eyes on familiar objects for not more than half-an-hour, the Third and I were told to go below and get on with certain jobs. We saw nothing wrong in this, but when five o'clock came and we were informed that we would have to work until midnight when our pay stopped, the Skipper and Chief were called names of which they would not have approved.

About seven o'clock a fireman came below and told me that my mother was ashore asking for me. When I reached the deck it was dusk, but light enough for me to recognise mother and wave to her. Permission to go ashore in a rowing boat for a half hour was refused. I took this rather badly, since apart from the desire to see mother again I was much concerned for her safety, because to reach home she had to pass through the slum part of the town where, to my personal knowledge, strange things happened after dark.

About a quarter-of-an-hour before midnight the Skipper and Chief came and stood at the top of the engine room, idly watching us less important members of the ship's company, working. For the last few minutes before midnight the Skipper held his watch in his hand and on the stroke of twelve bellowed "All hands knock-off."

After a week-end with my people I enrolled at the Marine School, South Shields, to prepare for my Second Class B.O.T. Certificate examination. The usual practice at that time was to take a two week course and then enter for the examination. Some sat the examination after a shorter time at school while others took much longer to fit themselves for the ordeal. It depended to a great extent upon the time and facilities afforded at sea for study. The decision as to when a student should present himself for examination rested with the school instructors.

After the second day's lectures I approached the senior lecturer, Mr. Peter Youngson, B.Sc., who was exceedingly popular because of his sympathetic understanding of a junior engineer's difficulties, and highly respected for his wide sea experience and advanced theoretical knowledge, with the suggestion that as the instruction given was not new to me, I should apply to sit for the examination right away. It was typical of the man to say that if I would stay behind after school hours with him he would put me to the test and find out if I required further tuition. Needless to say I readily agreed, and at eight o'clock that night he told me that I stood a good chance of getting through.

On the first three days of the week following I sat the examination and on the Friday learnt that I had passed. What a thrill ! Will I ever forget it ? After another free week-end with my family I applied to my old shipping company for a job, and was told that providing I would pay the train fare to Cardiff all they could offer me was Third on the *Duffield*, due to sail in two days' time.

To go back in the same ship was not to my liking, as apart from the rather unfair treatment I felt I had received, I wanted sea experience with other types of machinery, my ambition being to sail with steam turbines which were then being adopted for merchant ship propulsion. Such ships, however, were few and there were many young engineers with similar desires. Also, to turn down the job offered might mean that I would be weeks or perhaps months out of work, a state of affairs I could ill afford. I therefore re-joined my old ship as Third with a certain amount of apprehension.

Upon boarding the ship at Cardiff after sitting all night in the corner of a railway carriage, I found that all officers of the previous voyage, with the exception of the Third, were going back in the ship, this information was tendered by the Second, whom I met on the deck. In answer to my enquiry he said the Chief was in his cabin and that no doubt he would give me a right royal welcome. I took this to mean that I would be anything but welcome, so it was with considerable apprehension that I knocked on the Chief's cabin door. In answer to the loud, gruff "come in" I entered, and to my amazement and relief received a very warm greeting. I was even invited for the first time to sit down in his cabin.

We left the following day with our cargo of coal for Port Said and it was exactly thirteen months before the *Duffield* returned to home waters. At the end of that time I had no complaints regarding my treatment, and although I had to work just as hard as Third as I did as Fourth I could devote more time to my studies. What had happened to the old Chief during the fortnight I had been out of the ship I don't know, but he was a changed man. I could do no wrong, and even my endeavours to prevent the new Fourth being brow-beaten were not altogether unsuccessful.

Having served more than the twelve months' qualifying time in possession of my Second Class Certificate, I was eligible to sit the examination for a First Class Certificate, and I felt competent to do so without further tuition. This I did after being reassured by my good friend Peter Youngson, and at the end of the four days' examination was awarded my First Class Certificate.

CHAPTER V

THOSE EARLY MOTOR SHIPS

MY next ship was an oil tank steamer of about 7,000 tons dead-weight, my first experience of this type of ship. I signed on as Third Engineer. A few hours before sailing from the river Tyne the Second went sick, and as he was unable to proceed with the ship it was my good fortune to be promoted to Second the day after joining. To have achieved such a high rank so early in my career — I was then twenty-three years of age — was something to be proud of, but it was of course due to my good luck. I had, however, worked hard and obtained a First Class B.O.T. Certificate, which in those days a Second was expected to possess, otherwise sailing of the ship would have been delayed until the services of an older man were obtained.

After a successful voyage to U.S.A./Mediterranean/Black Sea/ U.K., the thought uppermost in my mind upon entering home waters was how the Second Engineer had fared during our absence. I can, perhaps, be forgiven for secretly hoping that he had secured another job in the meantime, or even, much to my shame, that he was not sufficiently recovered to re-join the ship. However, upon entering the dock I quickly spotted him with his kit-bag on the ground beside him, patiently waiting to come on board. This meant, of course, that I would have to revert to Third if I wished to stay in the ship.

It was a Saturday morning when we docked at Wallsend-on-Tyne and it was well into the afternoon before I was able to finish my work and go ashore for the twenty-four hours' leave allowed me. The nearest railway station, Point Pleasant, was small and hardly ever used outside factory hours. On the platform was one other passenger waiting for one of the infrequent trains, and although I recognised him at once, he was none other than Mr. Campbell, the highly respected Yard Manager of the Wallsend Slipway and Engineering Co., Ltd., he apparently did not remember me. As can be imagined, I was rather keen that he should recognise me for I was very proud of having, even if only for one voyage, sailed as Second.

As I stood on the platform my tall, lean, fresh complexioned, genial station companion, sauntered up and down, passing me when going in each direction. Once or twice I thought he was about to speak as he came abreast of me, but he always looked away and passed on. However, after passing by many times he stopped in front of me and said, " I seem to know your face but can't bring your name to mind," whereupon I eagerly replied " Yes, Sir, you know me, my name is Lamb." Apparently he had a better memory for faces than for names and at once remembered. He asked me what I had been doing since finishing my apprentice-ship and I told him I had been to sea.

He then asked, presumably with a view to making conversation, when I intended sitting for my Second-Class Certificate, to which I promptly replied with pride that I had obtained my First-Class Certificate and that I had made a voyage as Second. I went on to tell him the name of the ship and how I had come to serve as Second at such at early age, moreover, that the permanent Second had returned and that I had to revert to Third, to which he promptly retorted with a smile "And you don't like it." He then became more interested in the conversation, and just as the train drew into the station and he made for a First-Class compart-ment he said, " If you can get honourable release from your present job come and see me at nine o'clock on Monday morning and I'll give you a Second's berth on an eight-handed ship." This meant that the ship he had in mind carried eight engineers, which at that time indicated a very big ship and a very responsible position. My elation at such a prospect can be better imagined than described.

The problem then was to obtain honourable release from my present job, and as my ship was due to sail early on Monday morning I knew that this would be exceedingly difficult to get, particularly as Mr. Muir, the Superintendent attending my ship, was a difficult man to approach on any matter, let alone seek release and expect him to find a replacement over the week-end. However, the offer made by Mr. Campbell was so attractive that before going home I turned my steps in the direction of the Superintendent's home in Newcastle. On the way I decided, after many rejections, upon what I would say when Mr. Muir appeared before me, and then repeated it over and over again so that I would have no difficulty in saying my piece when the frightful moment arrived.

When in sight of the house my courage almost failed me, and there is no doubt that my knock on the door was very faint. It was evidently loud enough to be heard inside because the maid soon appeared and I told her I would like to speak to her Master. A moment or two later my Superintendent appeared, and his greeting in a loud and challenging voice which set my knees knocking was, " What do *you* want ? " Having forgotten completely my carefully prepared opening remarks, I told him in halting words about Mr. Campbell's offer. After listening with obvious impatience he dismissed me with the words " Certainly not, you have your twenty-four hours' leave and then get back to the ship," whereupon I raised my hat and bid him good afternoon, not altogether displeased that the interview was over even though I had not got what I so much desired.

Before I reached the gate, some dozen steps from the front door, he shouted " What are your intentions ? " The sound of his voice made me quake as I was unaware that he was still there. I replied that I was going home for the twenty hours that were left to me and that I would report for duty on Sunday evening and sail with the ship on Monday morning. This was evidently not the answer he expected, since he walked towards me and in a less unkindly voice said " Oh ! will you. Well in that case I think I might release you so that you can take Mr. Campbell's job, and the best of luck." Whether this kindly man with the formidable exterior heard my whispered thanks as he turned his back on me I will never know. This goes to show how deceptive outward appearances can be.

Needless to say I presented myself at Mr. Campbell's office well before the appointed time, and after waiting for what seemed like hours I was shown into his presence. He introduced me to his assistant and remarked " This is the young fellow I have selected

The sound of his voice made me quake.

The sound of his voice made me quake.

as Second for that motor job." The word "motor" conveyed nothing to me then. After being given instructions with regard to joining the ship, during which no mention was made of the type of machinery installed, I was dismissed.

I was very hesitant about asking any questions during the short interview, it being sufficient that I had been given the job, but being a budding engineer I was anxious to know the type of machinery I would find in the ship. Before reaching the office door I somehow managed to summon up sufficient courage to put the question uppermost in my mind. The answer I got was that she was a diesel job, at which my heart sank, because I had had no experience of such engines and I felt that the offer had been made to me under a misapprehension. However, although I would have given my right hand to get the job I felt that I could not accept, and said with reluctance, " I am sorry, Sir, but I don't know any-thing about diesel jobs," to which the reply came like a flash " Nor do I, nor does he, nor does anybody, but we have all got to learn. Do *you* want to learn ? " to which I quickly replied " I certainly do," and the reply seemed to satisfy Mr. Campbell, because he bade me good morning and turned his back on me.

I had some three weeks to wait before joining the m/s *San Sebastian* which was then under construction, and spent the time collecting every available piece of information about diesel engines. There wasn't much to be had at that time, but I managed to get hold of a copy of Supina's book on diesel engines and read and re-read it many times. Consequently, upon reaching the ship I felt that I knew a little about this new type of engine and hoped I would not appear too ignorant in the eyes of the engineers who were to serve under me. I was greatly relieved to find that the other engineers had had no previous experience either, the only one who knew anything at all, and that wasn't very much, being the Chief Engineer.

The 2000 horse-power main engines were of the two-cycle type designed to run at 160 r.p.m. The ship had twin screws, which was indeed fortunate, because the two engines were rarely in running order at the same time. Our troubles soon came along. They were so numerous and so serious that regular times for meals and sleep were out of the question. After three months we had reached a port in the Black Sea, loaded a cargo and had got as far as the Bay of Biscay on our way home when we had to " call it a day." No engineer had slept in his bunk for three weeks.

All spare parts, of which there were an abundance when the ship left, had been used up and all the tools were worn and of little use. Even the chain blocks had been strained through frequent usage to such an extent that they were unsafe. The truth of the statement that all spare parts had been used up and all tools worn out will not be questioned when it is mentioned that out of sixty-four crankshaft, crankpin and crosshead bearings, only five had not been remetalled during those never-to-be-forgotten three months. Every piston had been out several times to free piston rings and seven of the pistons had been renewed because the heads had fractured, whilst five cylinder covers had also cracked and had to be replaced by spare covers.

The engine followed steam engine practice inasmuch as it was of the open-fronted type and all bearings had to be lubricated by hand. The quantity of lubricating oil used per day was never less than a hundred gallons. Hundreds of barrels had to be emptied whilst on deck and the oil carried in buckets into the engine room. The bearings were very troublesome and the watch-keeping engineers had to be constantly on the alert for hot bearings. The senior engineer of the watch hadn't time for anything but ' feeling-round,' and with so much oil being thrown off the moving parts he had to wear oilskins and so'wester to avoid getting an oil bath every time he made his rounds.

The ship was towed home from the Bay of Biscay, and the owners decided that the engines were of no further use and new engines of a different type were installed. By the time the ship arrived in a home port we engineers had made up some of the sleep lost and had removed much of the grime from our bodies.

At that time starting air was generally stored in steel containers charged to a pressure of 1200 lbs. per square inch, and on one of the early motor ships in which I served the heads of the twelve ten-foot long and one-foot diameter containers were provided with fusible plugs. These plugs were, presumably, intended to melt and release the highly compressed air should a fire occur in the engine room, and so prevent the containers exploding. It is perhaps not so easy to understand now the reasoning which resulted in the fitting of these fusible plugs, but it must be remembered that such high pressures in marine practice were unknown at that time.

The ship had not been at sea a week before a report like a shot from a gun, followed by an ear piercing rush of air, was heard. While we were investigating the cause, a second fusible plug blew out and struck an auxiliary machine with terrific force. The second was followed by others, any of which would have killed a man instantly had it hit him. The engine room had to be evacuated, until one man volunteered to re-enter and release the compressed air from the remainder of the containers. Had such an act been carried out on the battlefield it would have merited the V.C. or other high decoration, but I don't remember this particular volunteer even being officially thanked!

At times I felt it was more than the human frame could stand, and would have followed my colleagues into steamships had I not become convinced that the diesel engine had a future. What impressed me most was the exceedingly low fuel consumption for the power developed, the absence of unpleasant boiler work and the comparatively cool engine room when compared with those of steamships.

My next three motorships belonged to the same owner, and although each engine was of a different make, all were of the 2-cycle open-fronted type. It now seems strange that designers persisted for so long in trying to make the diesel engine look as much like a steam engine as possible. Apart from a certain amount of prejudice to be overcome there would, I imagine, be some difficulty, as well as reluctance, in drilling holes through such large crankwebs and journals in order that forced lubrication could be employed.

One of these ships was engaged during the early part of the 1914/1918 war in carrying iron ore from Tunis to Middlesbrough, and although the engines were designed for 120 r.p.m., which would have given the ship a speed of 10 knots, it was impossible to operate at a speed greater than 90 r.p.m. Bearings began to heat up when a higher speed was attempted.

During five round voyages to Tunis at an average speed of only 6 knots, we saw nothing of submarines, even though most of the steaming was done in submarine infested waters. When approaching Middlesbrough on the sixth voyage, however, vigorous ringing of the engine room telegraph indicated that a submarine had been sighted by the look-out on the bridge and that more speed was required. Whilst being desirous of giving more speed, we were much concerned about what we knew would happen to the engine. However, the speed control lever was advanced a little at a time and very soon there was a suspicious smell. A few moments later, smoke began to rise from some of the bearings, and although the Skipper was told that bearings were running hot, more speed and still more speed was requested. The engine revolutions went up to about 100, the highest ever recorded, and after twenty minutes or so the port engine was making so much noise and was enveloped in so much smoke that it had to be stopped, submarine or no submarine. Soon afterwards the starboard engine had to be stopped for the same reason.

As nothing more could be done with the engines I went on deck to see what was happening, and there was the bold submarine rapidly overtaking us from astern. As it passed the White Ensign was clearly visible, and the Commander shouted " What the h . . . are you loitering about here for ? " The retort of our angry Skipper can be left to the imagination. To have his engines ruined was bad enough, but the realisation that we had not been chased by a German submarine was too much ! As it was quite out of the question to run the engines, we drifted into Bridlington Bay until tugs were sent out to tow us into port.

Upon reaching port I was sent to join another motorship, which was then at the Builder's yard. Construction had been completed some weeks before and during those weeks repeated attempts had been made to get the engine working. Success had not attended these efforts when I arrived, and in answer to questions I was told that whilst the engine would start up satisfactorily on compressed air, it stopped immediately the control lever was put into the " On fuel " position.

At that time diesel fuel was looked upon as a heavy fuel for that particular type of engine and those in charge of the tests had decided that the oil was too heavy to ignite, so the fuel tanks were filled with paraffin. Paraffin did not give the desired results but the attempts to start the engine continued until I joined the ship.

An examination of the engine disclosed that the camshaft was driven by the crankshaft through a dog-clutch which had thirty degrees play between the teeth. The purpose of this was to bring the camshaft into the correct position for reverse running. It was also found that the spring holding the two parts of the dog-clutch together was not strong enough to keep them in the same relative positions whilst the engine was in motion, and that this was the reason why the engine had not started running on fuel. This fault caused the camshaft to " hunt," and instead of fuel being injected near the top centre it was being injected thirty degrees or so after that position.

As a stronger spring was not immediately available it was decided to secure the two halves of the dog-clutch in their correct relative positions for one direction of rotation only, in order to get the engine working and prove that this was the cause of the trouble. By that time no-one belonging to the shore staff had any confidence in the results. I was quite sure, however, that the engine would work, but not prepared for what did actually happen.

As soon as the starting lever was moved to the " On fuel " position there was a terrific explosion and dense smoke filled the engine room, proving beyond all doubt that the fuel had ignited. After the smoke had cleared, the exhaust pipe of the engine was observed to be completely wrecked, and upon going on deck for fresh air we found that the funnel, and with it the silencer, had been displaced and was lying at an angle of about forty-five degrees from the vertical. Within half-an-hour fire and police boats began converging from all directions. They had been told that the explosion was so violent that many must have been killed or burnt by the flames which shot a hundred feet into the air.

Upon investigating the cause of the explosion, it was found that the diesel fuel and paraffin which had been injected into the cylinders during the weeks preceding had accumulated in the exhaust pipe of this two-cycle engine, and when the engine did begin working on fuel the hot gases from the cylinders ignited the large quantities of fuel lying in the exhaust pipe.

In another motorship difficulty was experienced in keeping the bearings down to normal running temperature due to the surfaces being too small for the load carried. Being open-fronted, the arrangement for lubricating the bearings comprised innumerable oil boxes working on the siphon principle, situated high up in the engine room. In practice it was found that the siphons were quite unable to supply sufficient oil, and the lubrication had to be done by constantly pouring oil into the boxes and causing it to overflow into the pipes connected to the bearings. The oil had to be carried from the storage tanks in buckets, so the greasers didn't have much spare time during their watches.

In an endeavour to improve matters, someone in the design office got the idea of cutting four equally spaced flats on each crankshaft journal, the idea being to carry the oil introduced by hand through an opening at the top, round to the bottom halves of the bearings, which in two-cycle engines are under constant high pressure.

The pipes originally intended to convey the oil from the boxes to the crankshaft bearings were connected to the underside of the bearings, and the effect of cutting flats on the shaft journals was to carry the oil introduced by hand round to the bottom half of the bearings as desired, but what was not anticipated was that the flats had a pumping action and the oil introduced at the top of the bearings was discharged to the boxes high up in the engine room. The boxes quickly overflowed, and the engine had to be stopped and the holes in the bearings plugged before the ship could sail.

This idea having proved worthless, it was then decided to lubricate the bearings by grease, and accordingly innumerable ratchet-operated lubricators were provided, together with pipes for conveying the grease to the bearings. This idea improved the running of the bearings slightly but resulted in almost intolerable conditions in the engine room. Even with grease lubrication the bearings ran at too high a temperature, and when it is remembered that all principle bearings had to be felt by hand regularly and frequently, the ingenuity which had to be displayed to avoid getting the eyes filled with grease thrown off the revolving cranks will be appreciated. To many present-day engineers the statement that engineers had to keep watches in oilskins, gumboots and goggles will seem almost incredible, but such was the lot of the pioneer diesel engineers.

One of my biggest jobs in those early motorships occurred when in the Indian Ocean. At the time the twin two-cycle type engines were working fairly well, when without warning a heavy thumping emanated from the starboard engine, which quickly lost speed and then abruptly stopped. The turning gear was at once engaged but it was found impossible to move the crankshaft.

Our first thought was that something had got round the propeller, and to check this the engine was disconnected from the propeller shaft, a job that kept all hands busy for nine hours swinging 14 lb. hammers in an engine room temperature of 110°F. Even then the engine could not be moved, and the next guess was that a piston had seized. Before we had time to verify this the port engine behaved similarly, and when our investigation had been completed, it was found that the piston cooling water to each of the pistons was being short circuited in varying amounts, and later it was found that this was due to the steel internal pipes in the piston rods having corroded away.

This installation comprised eight cylinders, and as there were only two spare internal pipes on board there was nothing for it but to make pipes cut from various parts of the engine and deck piping systems which could, on a pinch, be done without. This incident occurred during very hot weather and the repair took twenty-two days, the entire engine room staff working six hours on and four hours off duty. In the twenty-two days the ship drifted nearly six hundred miles, but the work was ultimately accomplished and the temporary pipes served the purpose until the ship returned to a home port.

I could go on writing about the incidents which occurred in

those early motorships, most of them being sunk by the enemy during the 1914/18 war, but too much space would be required and, besides, some of the narratives would now seem so fantastic that they may be considered untrue, or at any rate much exaggerated.

In view of the hard manual work, long hours each day in the engine room, lack of sleep, bruised body and cut hands, carbon embedded in the skin and no time for anything in port except work and sleep, the difficulty experienced by the owners to man those early motorships with the right type of engineers is understandable.

Added to all these hardships was the mental strain endured, for it must be remembered that those engineers were dealing with temperatures and pressures greatly in excess of anything previously experienced, as well as the ever-present possibility of meeting a violent end as a result of explosions in engine exhaust pipes, scavenge air ducts and air compressors. Fire also was " just round the corner " as it were, because in many cases the engines ran on low viscosity gas oil which leaked all too frequently from improperly made or badly designed joints of high-pressure pipes. The oil from these joints was projected with great force in the form of fine sprays, which could not be seen but could be easily ignited. One ship at least was burnt out by such a spray striking the engine's hot exhaust pipe.

With very few exceptions the engineers who found themselves in motorships got out at the very first opportunity, because they thought diesel engines had no future and didn't see the sense of working so hard under such conditions for something that would not come to anything. Holding the opposite view I stuck to motorships. This wasn't easy, as at that time the total number afloat could be counted on the fingers, and several times I had to accept a lower rank at reduced wages in order to get experience of the six types then in existence, namely, Carel, Polar-Atlas, Burmeister & Wain, Sulzer, Werkspoor and the German M.A.N.

Being so keen on diesel engines and so confident that they offered me the opportunity I desired so earnestly, I made copious notes of anything unusual which happened and appended my views as to the cause. Some of the views were, I found later, wide of the mark, but as something unusual happened almost every hour of the day my endeavours to answer the question " Why ? " resulted in acquiring knowledge which I would not have acquired had I been content to accept everything as inevitable. Also I chased everything that had been written by others, and read and re-read until I had not only memorised what had been written, but knew what the writer was thinking. The only book available at that time was Professor Supino's *Land and Marine Diesel Engines*. I knew the contents of this 700 page book so well that I had no difficulty in finding at once the page dealing with any particular part of the subject.

It has been most gratifying to watch the development of the diesel engine from the stage I have endeavoured to describe, to the highly efficient and trouble-free product of today. No one can claim to have been responsible for its success. Credit must go to a great army of designers, engine manufacturers and a lesser number of shipowners who had the courage to invest their money in ships which could not be expected to make a profit.

That the diesel engine should have to be provided with a high grade and consequently expensive fuel did not, to my mind, seem right, as the thermodynamics of the diesel cycle provided all that was required to burn cheaper fuels. This was generally recognised and many unsuccessful attempts to solve the problem were made during the first forty years of the engine's commercial life. Having during recent years been able to make a major contribution to the complete solution of this problem, my efforts are now concerned with the development of the marine internal combustion turbine, commonly called the gas turbine, which will eventually supersede the diesel engine just as the diesel engine superseded the steam reciprocating engine during the early part of the present century.

CHAPTER VI

A SLEEPY STORY

AT one period during my early twenty's I served in an old
tramp steamer which most people thought unworthy of a
second glance, but never did I see a more attractive engine room
than the one in that particular ship. It was not outstanding
because of the type of machinery it contained, as this was the same
as in hundreds of other ships. It was because the engine room and
everything in it was so spick and span. All machined steel and
brass surfaces of the machinery were highly polished, copper
pipes shone with a brilliance equal to mother's ornamental copper
kettle, while the paint on the bulkheads always appeared fresh.
Even the chequered steel floor plates, gratings and ladders were
so clean that to sit on them wouldn't have soiled white trousers.

I doubt if there was a cleaner and better kept engine room anywhere, the credit for which must go to a short wiry Scot who was
Second Engineer. When not eating or sleeping " Sandy " could
always be found busily engaged removing specks of dirt or stains
from the polished parts. Had he been married I am afraid his
wife would have had a harassing time during his periods ashore.

The part the Third and Fourth engineers had to play in maintaining the cleanliness of this model engine room was to make
sure that at the end of each watch every movable thing was in its
proper place, that not a single match-stick or cigarette end could
be found, not even on the polished brass ash tray which graced
the small scrubbed-to-white desk, that no drop of oil or water
was where it should not be, and that all iron filings and the like
had been removed from the vice bench. In short, everything had
to be in the same place and in the same condition as when Sandy
left it.

This wasn't so easy as might appear, because for reasons of
economy the engine room was only dimly lighted by three permanent paraffin oil lamps and one portable colza lamp, none of
which had the power of more than a couple of candles, and the

Fourth and I finished our p.m. watches during the hours of darkness. Should we have the misfortune to overlook anything at the end of a watch, Sandy would wait until he thought the culprit was sound asleep and then rudely awaken him with orders to go below and remove the cause of his displeasure. On one occasion such treatment was meted out to me because I had inadvertently left the lid of a locker open.

Sandy's constant fear was that rain or sea spray would enter the engine room and spoil his good work. The result was that he would never allow the skylights to be opened fully, so that the temperature was always higher than it might have been. In the tropics the heat was almost unbearable, the temperature at the coolest part of the engine room being frequently 120°F.

Being young and healthy and having to work hard with the tools between my day watches, it was only with the greatest difficulty that I could keep awake in such heat and semi-darkness during my p.m. watch, which began at midnight. To do so I had to do all sorts of physical jerks, such as hanging on to gratings and swinging along hand over hand. To make matters worse, the silent-running engine gave no trouble so long as the bearings were oiled regularly every half-hour. In the intervals there was nothing to do but walk to and fro and try to keep awake.

The Chief would not allow us to do jobs either for the ship or ourselves during the night watches in case some part of our routine duties got neglected, so this possible remedy was denied me. Only those who have tried to keep awake under such conditions will appreciate how difficult it is to do so. The eye-lids feel as though they have lead weights hanging on to them. To sit down or even stand still for a few minutes would be fatal, so there was nothing for it but to keep on the move. In spite of my efforts to ward off sleep I often came into violent contact with the bulkheads at each end of my promenade.

At the beginning of one voyage a young Welshman, who was quickly named " Taffy," joined the ship as Fourth Engineer. He was capable and a good shipmate, but like myself he found Sandy's views about the condition in which the engine room was to be kept a bit irksome. He, too, had great difficulty in keeping awake during his night watch, which was from 8 p.m. till mid-night, when I took over from him. Poor Taffy was hauled out of his bunk many times at four o'clock in the morning during the first week or two. I saved him on several occasions, but some-times things he had done or had not done escaped my notice, being half asleep and not nearly so vigilant as Sandy.

Once when I went down below at midnight to take over my watch I found Taffy vigorously trying to remove with a scrubbing brush a huge smudge from the otherwise lily-white boiler bulk-head. At first I thought I must be dreaming, as such a blemish in that engine room was unbelievable. Taffy's excited demeanour and his calls for help, however, soon convinced me that I was awake. In answer to my enquiry as to how such an awful thing had happened I was told that he had accidentally upset the black oil can.

In my half dazed state this seemed a perfectly feasible explan-ation, as the black oil can was a tin vessel of about one gallon capacity containing thick black oil used for lubricating the piston rods, the practice being to apply the oil by means of a swab brush not unlike a long handled tar brush. I therefore did all I could to help my distressed shipmate to remove the smudge, but it was soon apparent that nothing short of a coat of paint would hide it. Upon promising to do what I could during my watch to make the smudge less prominent, Taffy went off to his cabin to lie awake, so he told me later, waiting for the explosion which he knew would occur when Sandy went below at 4 a.m. to take over from me.

The effort put forward to remove the smudge awakened me fully and I endeavoured to reconstruct the scene at the moment the black oil can was upset. The usual place for the can was on the middle grating between the high-pressure and intermediate-pressure cylinder columns. Had it upset whilst in that position the mess would have been on the bottom platform and would have been easily cleaned up. To smudge the boiler bulkhead the can would have to be upset when on the top grating, and I couldn't conceive any reason for taking it up there. From my reasoning I could only conclude that Taffy hadn't spoken truly.

At first I thought I was dreaming.

The only portable lamp allowed hung between the high-pressure and intermediate-pressure piston rods, and whilst working at the smudge I noticed that this lamp caused the shadow of the moving high-pressure piston rod and crosshead to be projected on to the boiler bulkhead right in the middle of the smudge. In a flash I could see what had happened. Poor Taffy had been more asleep than awake when he made his last oiling, and instead swabbing the piston rod he had swabbed its shadow !

At eight bells (4 a.m.) down came Sandy in his usual spruce and sprightly manner. He was a remarkable chap. Although his age was greater than Taffy's and mine put together he was just as active as either, and was always as wide awake at four o'clock in the morning as he was at that time in the afternoon. Neither early rising nor the heat in the engine room seemed to trouble him, although when it came to hard work he made sure that the young fellows did their full share and some more.

I watched Sandy, with more apprehension than usual, as he descended the ladder on that eventful morning. When he reached the middle grating his eyes turned, it seemed instinctively, towards the boiler bulkhead. He stood staring at it for a full half minute, and if he had not been as bald as a billiard ball I would have expected his hair to stand on end. Instead of walking along the grating to have a closer view, he came down the last ladder at speed and made straight for me. I thought he was going to hit me, but he didn't. The poor man just stood before me pointing to the smudge, his face as white as the bulkhead should have been. He was quite speechless, and in answer to the plain question in his eyes I shook my head.

Sandy swung round and shot up the ladders three steps at a time. A minute or so afterwards Taffy, in pyjamas and looking very dejected, was being literally driven down the ladders. Sandy had got his voice back in full measure, but it wouldn't be discreet to record what he said as he helped Taffy down with his foot. Taffy was ordered to get busy and remove the smudge, but after much talking I convinced Sandy that it wouldn't come off and that it would have to be painted over. " Right," he said, " you will both start painting at 8.30 a.m. and you won't stop, not even for meals, until the whole of the bulkhead has been painted." We finished the job at 9 o'clock that night, but the Chief Engineer, who thought the punishment too severe, intervened and we had our meals.

CHAPTER VII

HAZARDS OF THE SEA

DURING my fouteen years at sea in general cargo ships and oil tankers I experienced a fair share of rough weather. Often did I have an unpleasant feeling in the middle region, but I still don't know what it is like to be really seasick. In consequence I am afraid I didn't always fully sympathise with my shipmates so affected, when in all seriousness they wished the ship would sink if nothing less would stop her rolling and pitching.

My worst storm was encountered during the early part of my sea career. We had loaded rice at Bassein, Burma, for U.K. and had a perfectly smooth passage to Suez and, of course, through the Suez Canal. Soon after leaving Port Said in the month of November we ran into bad weather. which rapidly got worse as we proceeded in the direction of Malta. Under conditions normally encountered in that part of the world the distance of just under a thousand miles between these two places would have been covered in less than five days, but on this occasion Malta was not sighted until sixteen days after leaving Port Said. The gale which we experienced was wide-spread and several ships foundered in the Mediterranean and the Atlantic.

Our relatively small ship named the *s/s Garfield* of about 7,000 tons deadweight, was of the turret deck type, a type abandoned many years ago. Instead of the sides of the ship being straight all the way down, or almost so, the upper portion extended vertically downwards from the deck to within a couple of feet of the water line. At this point the hull turned outwards for about six feet, after which it continued vertically downward, the horizontal portions on each side being called the turret decks.

Such ships in cross-section looked very much like the upper half of a bottle, the neck of the bottle representing the part of the ship above the turret decks. The result was that when the ship rolled in a heavy sea the flat turret decks on each side became submerged in turn, and owing to the weight of water, amounting to hundreds of tons, on these decks the ship would take an unusually long time to return to the upright position.

It took very little to start our ship rolling and keep on rolling. Rough seas made her roll through a much greater angle than the more orthodox type of ship, and whilst the speed of the roll when one of the turret decks was under water was slow, it increased rapidly immediately the deck rose above the surface of the sea. As can be imagined, this two speed roll made life on board extremely uncomfortable. Even those who had spent most of their lives at sea had difficulty in getting around.

When a ship left port in those days all communication with the outside world, apart from passing ships, was severed. Wireless had been invented but only the largest passenger ships had been equipped with this means of communication. When, therefore, we left Port Said all we knew was that we were running into bad weather. How long it would last or how bad it would get was not for us to know. The Skipper thought the gale would blow itself out in a day or so, but he proved a bad forecaster. The weather got steadily worse, and at the end of the first twenty-four hours we had covered only seventy miles, which was about one-third of our normal day's performance.

On the second night out the wind velocity increased so much that movement about the decks was possible only by grimly holding on to the handrails and hauling oneself along hand over hand. The howling wind completely drowned the loudest of voices and to release one's hold even for a second could have only one result. One of our two deck apprentices was washed overboard unseen and unheard that night. I forget his name, but remember that he was a popular boy and his disappearance was a great shock to us all.

During the next few days the wind and sea didn't vary, either for better or worse — some old sailors said it couldn't possibly be worse. Everything not firmly secured was washed overboard. The two lifeboats were saved only by lashing them so securely that it is doubtful if they could have been launched in an emergency, even if it had been possible to manage them in such a rough sea. All cabins opening on to the deck were flooded and regular meals had to be abandoned. The galley was put out of action and the only available food consisted of hard ships' biscuits and water to soften and wash them down. Before the vegetable locker was washed overboard we could supplement our meagre diet by boiling potatoes in the engine room.

The ship was not fitted with electric lighting, so oil lamps were used for navigation lights. After the oil in the mast head lights was consumed, on the third or fourth day, it was impossible to stay on deck long enough to lower the burnt-out lamp and replace it without the grave risk of being washed overboard. Several attempts made nearly ended in another tragedy. It probably didn't matter anyway, as the speed of our ship and all others in the vicinity would be too slow to enable them to take evasive action with a view to preventing a collision. Strangely enough I don't think anyone gave a thought to the possibility of another ship running into us in the black darkness.

The engine room skylights were not closed before seas were sweeping over the ship, and then it was too late. The result was that much sea water entered the engine room each time the ship rolled. Being a steam engine, most of the water landed on the hot cylinder tops and steam pipes and was at once converted into steam. This at times reduced visibility so much that it was difficult and dangerous to get around and tend the engines, which in the circumstances, required more than usual attention.

During the early part of the gale the speed governor on the engine broke beyond repair and the engine had then to be governed by hand. The drill was that as the ship's stem rose to an oncoming wave and the stern went down and down, the hand throttle had to be opened at a certain rate in order to give the engine more steam. Without more steam the engine would have stopped due to the propeller being deeply submerged. Then as the wave passed under the ship and the stern rose, the throttle had to be slowly closed to prevent the engine racing and risking a breakdown. If closed too quickly the engine would stop. As the stem of the ship went down into the trough of the waves and the propeller rose clear of the sea, it was a signal to rush to the side of the engine room to avoid being scalded by the sea water that got well heated by contact with the hot engine cylinders and steam pipes on its way down.

All this had to be gone through every fifteen to twenty seconds. We in the engine room were sheltered from the sixty mile an hour wind sweeping the decks it is true, but the rolling and pitching ship made it hazardous to let go of some rigid part of the engine or ship's structure. The steel floor plates were covered with oil thrown off the revolving parts of the engine and water which came through the skylights, so that had they been covered with ice it couldn't have been more difficult to stand on one's feet. When shelter from the hot falling water had to be sought it wasn't a case of running the fifteen or twenty feet across a clear floor. All one had to do was to let go and the movement of the ship and the greasy floor would get one there in record time. The outward slide was stopped by crashing into the bulkhead and grabbing hold of a vice bench attached to it. The slide in the opposite direction was towards the engine, and time and again the momentum was so great that I miraculously avoided being thrown into the engine crankpit, where I would have been pounded to pulp in no time.

During this time the watches were double-banked, which is sea parlance and means that the number of engineers and firemen on duty at the same time was doubled and they worked six hours on watch and six hours off. In the case of this ship it meant two engineers and three firemen on each watch. Five men were little enough to do all there was to do in the circumstances. Heavy rolling and pitching made the firing of the two three-furnace boilers and the oiling of the engine difficult and hazardous, while coal and ashes were flung into the wings of the stokehold.

This entailed a great deal of what is commonly called " bilge diving " to keep the pump suctions clear, and so prevent the water in the stokehold rising to a dangerous level. The bilge suctions in this ship, built before I was born, were situated in the most awkward positions. There was one at either side of the stokehold, both some four feet below the floor plates. To reach a point immediately above a suction, which was the nearest one could get to the suctions, one had to crawl through an opening about fifteen feet long, and just large enough to wriggle through, between the boiler and the bunker bulkhead. Whilst lying face downwards the suction had to be blindly prodded with an iron rod so that the coal, ashes, pieces of wood and chunks of oily waste would be dislodged and allow the water to flow into the pipe, thence to the pump and overboard.

On occasions the efforts would not be successful and the water would rise above the floor plates, flowing in a torrent from side to side as the ship rolled. It was then necessary for one of us to be lowered into the bilge until only head and shoulders protruded above the cold, black, slimy water. The drill then was to wait until the ship rolled in the opposite direction, when much of the water would leave the bilge and rush with a deafening roar to the other side of the ship. In the few seconds between the bilge being almost clear of water and the ship beginning the return roll the one whose turn it was had to drop quickly on to his knees, clear as much of the obstruction as possible with his hands and rise into an upright position before the roaring, rushing water could submerge him. Sometimes this cycle of operations had to be repeated a dozen times before the pumps began drawing the water and pumping it overboard.

When about twelve days out from Port Said a crack about two foot long was found extending from the top of the bulwark on one side of the ship. When I saw the crack, it was opening about a quarter of an inch each time a wave passed under the ship, and it was apparent to all that if the crack continued, the ship, which was then groaning ominously, would eventually break in two and founder. All sorts of suggestions were made, but the only practical one emanated from the Chief Engineer. It was to drill an inch diameter hole just ahead of the end of the gradually extending crack, so that it would run into the hole and perhaps go no further.

In ordinary weather the hole would have been drilled in the matter of an hour by a couple of men, but in the circumstances the half-inch thick steel plate was penetrated only after twenty-four hours' hard and hazardous work. During this time several of the men were badly hurt by being thrown violently against parts of the ship by waves as they came on board, even though the ship was hove-to.

Engineers were required for this work, but my orders were to remain below with one fireman and keep the engine turning at a speed sufficient to hold the ship head-on to the sea. Just what happened down below during those twenty-four hours will be left to the imagination, as it would take too long to describe how on many occasions the boilers were saved in the nick of time from running short of water, and the engines from stalling from want of steam because the bilge pump suctions required so much attention.

On the fourteenth day out from Port Said the storm began to abate, and two days later we steamed slowly into Valletta harbour, Malta's principal port, and dropped anchor. There is nothing attractive about the noise of an anchor being " let-go " but on that occasion the rattle of the chains was as sweet music to our ears, which for so long had heard nothing but howling wind with occasional crashes as one more fitting was wrenched from its fastenings and thrown from side to side of the ship before being washed overboard.

The ship was indeed a sorry sight. The decks were a shambles. The derricks, ventilators and other deck fittings that had not been torn down and thrown overboard were twisted into fantastic shapes and lying at all sorts of crazy angles. The deformed steel sides of deck houses and engine casings had the appearance of having been repeatedly struck by battering rams. The ship was rusted from end to end, most of the paint having been rubbed off by the scouring action of the thousands of tons of sea water that had struck the ship with terrific force during those never to be forgotten days and nights.

Temporary repairs were carried out to the fractured hull and machinery, the bilges cleared of coal and ashes, stocks of fresh water and food replenished, the injured put into hospital and other things done to enable the ship to steam the fifteen days which separated us from the nearest home port. Apart from a couple of days of bad weather in the Bay of Biscay, the voyage from Malta to the U.K. was uneventful. The bagged rice cargo, which had to be discharged by shore cranes because the ship's cargo handling gear was quite incapable, was found to be in surprisingly good condition. Less than five per cent. had been damaged by sea water which had found its way through hatches and strained seams in the ship's structure.

There is a saying about rats leaving a sinking ship, and I wonder if what happened on this ship during the storm confirms the saying. The ship was the home of many rats. We didn't see much of them in the engine room if they could get water to drink elsewhere, but there were plenty of them in the sixty foot long, five foot high tunnel between the engine room and the propeller shaft. The entire length of this tunnel had to be inspected at the end of each watch, and more often if anything went wrong with the shaft bearings. It was nothing to see a score or more rats scamper away from the rays of the colza oil lamp one had to carry. At normal times the rats seemed to have all they required in the shaft tunnel, but during the first six or seven days of the gale, numbers of them ventured into the engine room. Many were seen on the ladders and upper gratings and the assumption was that they were making for the deck. Whether they left the ship or not I cannot say, but it is a fact that at the end of the gale the number of rats in the tunnel had been reduced considerably.

CHAPTER VIII

THE ADVENTURES OF A GLASS EYE

AT the beginning of 1917 I joined a 10,000 ton deadweight motorship named *Kangaroo* whilst she was loading a cargo in the London Docks for the Middle East theatre of war. The outward appearance of this ship was unusual because she had no funnel. The exhaust gases from the two main and the three auxiliary diesel oil engines passed to atmosphere through pipes attached to the aftermost of the two masts. There was no boiler on board, all auxiliaries being driven electrically.

I had then been wearing an artificial eye for well over a year, but still had a desire to conceal the fact. Why, it is just a little difficult to say, because men were losing arms, legs, and eyes too, every day at that time. A missing arm or leg couldn't, of course, be concealed for long, and, besides, those who had been unfortunate enough to lose such a limb didn't make any attempt to hide the fact. With an eye it was different, or so it was to me.

I well remember boarding a tramcar in Leeds one morning and finding to my consternation that I had forgotten to put in my glass eye. The tram hadn't gone far fortunately when I made the discovery, and I jumped off at the next stop to go back for my eye, taking care to keep my head turned in such a way that my deficiency would not be noticed by the conductress or the other passengers. It may sound silly, but I was too conscious of my appearance to take another tram back, so I walked, endeavouring to keep my vacant socket from the gaze of people I passed.

In explanation of such conduct I can only say that I was quite young at the time and many music hall songs and gags referred to one-eyed blokes. Also, at that time, a serial story upon the life of Charlie Peace, who was executed years before in Leeds jail, was running in one of the Sunday newspapers, and I had read that the success of that scoundrel in avoiding just punishment for so long was attributed in some measure to his ability to alter his facial expression, and that in this he was assisted by his artificial eye !

My glass eye had to be taken out each night otherwise the eye-lids became very sore, and at first it was quite a problem to know just where to put it for safety, as a glass eye is very fragile. At sea it was an even greater problem, not only because a ship sometimes rolls, but when I joined the *Kangaroo*, the ship in which the following incident occurred, we were still at war and ships were being sunk by the enemy without warning ; 1917 was in fact a very black year for us. When I turned-in each night my concern was, therefore, to leave my glass eye where it would be safe and yet easy to find should the ship be torpedoed and, maybe, plunged into darkness, as I feared to abandon ship and find myself in a lifeboat and eventually going ashore without my glass eye where it ought to be.

Twenty hours after leaving London the *Kangaroo* was proceeding unescorted down the English Channel. The time was shortly after midnight, and having bathed and donned pyjamas I was in the act of jumping into my bunk in the usual sailor fashion, that is standing on the floor back to bunk with hands on bunk board. At that moment there was a deafening explosion and the ship trembled, as ships do when struck by a torpedo. A great many electric lamps were broken and extinguished by the shock, plunging the ship into semi-darkness. What happened during the next few seconds is a blank, but within a very short time I found myself in the engine room and remember being glad that I had had the presence of mind, or was it good luck, to slip my feet into a pair of strong shoes. Strangely enough I don't think I remembered my glass eye at that moment.

Where the torpedo had struck I did not then know, but water was pouring into the engine room, darkened by broken lamps and steam, through the starboard side of the ship. As the three large electrical generators, without which the ship would be helpless, were on that side of the engine room, I directed that all efforts should be concentrated upon preventing the inrushing water from splashing on to the dynamos.

Every bit of sacking, canvas and tarpaulin that could be procured was quickly brought, and with all possible haste and total disregard for their safety the engineers and greasers climbed and clung to pipes and parts of the ship's structure high up above the moving machinery to place the tarpaulins, etc. in positions which would protect the dynamos from the water. Monkeys could not have shown more agility than those men as they swung themselves in mid-air amidst the network of pipes. Moreover, many of the pipes contained exhaust gases from the oil engines, and that they were hot was evidenced later by the pitiful condition of their hands, arms and legs, which were literally covered with burns and blisters.

As the men high up in the darkened engine room could not see when they had got the tarpaulin, sacking or canvas in the best position, I stood near the dynamos and shouted directions. To make myself heard above the din of the machinery by men so far off was not easy, and after a time I began to lose my voice. I then began coughing, and when it seemed that I must choke, one violent cough brought something hard into my mouth, and by feeling with my tongue I knew it was my glass eye, which I had almost, but not quite, swallowed ! How it got there I don't know, but the assumption is that before I left my cabin I did two things, one was to slip my feet into shoes and the other to pick up my glass eye and put it into my mouth, where it would be safe during the emergency and available in the event of having to abandon ship.

In the dim light it was impossible to assess the damage to the ship, or even to form any ideas as to how much water was pouring in, as it was impossible to get near enough to the damaged ship's side with eyes open. It was, however, evident that the torpedo had not struck the engine room and it was assumed that the main damage was either just forward or just abaft that space, and that the impact had caused the seams and rivets in way of the engine room to leak badly.

After seeing that the dynamos were protected from the water as well as possible in the circumstances, I became conscious of the water having risen above the floor plates. The bilge pumps were already doing their duty, but the rate at which the water was coming in was obviously beyond their capacity. The large ballast pump and every other pump that could be connected to the bilges were quickly set to work, but the water level continued to rise. When well above the ankles I became very worried, because if the level got any higher, salt water would not only put the dynamos out of action, but the main engines also would stop, and that would be the end.

The Skipper sent a message to say that he was making for a suitable part of the coast on which to beach the ship, and to do everything humanly possible to keep the engines working a little longer. This message suggested that the ship was sinking, in which case the engines had to be kept going at all costs, and unless we could stop the water coming in or pump it out as fast as it came in, it would not be humanly possible to keep the engines operating. The first might have been accomplished by spreading and dropping a collision mat over the ship's damaged side, if we had had such a thing large enough, or if it had been wise to use lights so that the men could see what they were doing. For all we knew the enemy submarine responsible for our predicament was trailing us and waiting for an indication of our whereabouts so that he could come in and kill.

Our only hope, therefore, was to try and pump out faster. I had no idea of the rate at which the water was coming in nor of the rate at which we were pumping out. I did know, however, that the total rated capacity of the pumps then working was some 500 tons per hour, but who, in the circumstances, could say that the pumps were working at their maximum output ? For all we could tell some of the suction strums were partially choked or the pumps air-locked.

The only way to make sure that choked suction strums were not reducing the output of the pumps was to disconnect the suction pipes at points near the pumps, but as the suction pipes were well below the level of the water this wasn't easy. Somebody then got a bright idea. It was to open the watertight door at the entrance to the propeller shaft tunnel and allow the water to flow into that space. This was no sooner suggested than it was done, and being a twin-screw ship the large tunnel took away so much water from the engine room that the level fell sufficiently to enable us to land blows with heavy hammers on the suction pipes. No pipe could withstand for long such blows as were rained upon them that night. The breaking of the suction pipes proved a wise move, because although the amount of water in the engine room was not reduced, the height did not increase so rapidly. Our thoughts then turned to the sanitary pump and the main engine (diesel) cylinder jacket pumps which had a combined capacity of about 500 tons an hour.

Both these pumps were drawing from the sea and discharging the water overboard after circulating their respective parts of the machinery. If, therefore, these pumps could be made to draw their water from the engine room instead of the sea our salvage equipment would be augmented by 500 tons per hour, which it was estimated would stop the water level rising if it did not lower it.

A difficulty in giving effect to this idea was that the sea suction valves situated in the bilges could not be closed until the holes in the suction pipes had been made large enough for the pumps to draw their supply through them. Moreover, the instant this occurred the suction valves ought to be closed, otherwise the quantity of water entering the engine room would be greatly increased and the ship would indeed be lost.

However, a plan was worked out in a much shorter time than it would take to tell and soon we were pumping out at something in the region of 1,000 tons an hour. Whatever the exact figure was, it was certainly greater than the rate at which the water entered the engine room, because after a time the level was observed to be falling. Our spirits shot up to great heights when this became apparent and one man was so overcome that he wanted to embrace me. I was not in such an affectionate mood because my mind was busy trying to find the answer to the question " where do we stand if the level of water falls below the broken main engine suction pipes ? "

I must have relaxed for a moment because I remember being amused at the appearance of the men around me — some twenty of them — mostly stripped to the waist like myself, (I discarded my pyjama jacket quite early in the proceedings) and covered all over in black slime which had floated up from the bilges and was being thrown in all directions by the revolving flywheels, the lower parts of which were well under water.

All hands were having a little respite at that moment, the first for about four hours. Some of the men were examining the burns and cuts on their bodies while others were wiping the slime from one another's eyes. I was leaning against something near the main engine controls and trying to decide upon the action to be taken in the event of the water level falling below the main engine pump suctions. If this happened it would put the engines out of action.

As the water level fell the auxiliary pumps were shut off. But the level continued to fall although at a slower rate, so there was nothing for it but to open the main sea suction and allow more water to enter the engine room! I manipulated the sea valves myself on this occasion, and as I was groping my way back to the platform — the water was raining down so heavily over the spot where the sea valves were situated that it was impossible to see — I thought to myself " that water is warmer than I would have expected."

There was not time to think of the reason because at that moment the " beat " of one main engine changed, and when I got back to the control station it was evident that the port engine was gradually losing speed. " Short of fuel " was my first thought, spoken aloud, and up the ladder shot one of the junior engineers to change over the fuel tanks situated high up in the engine room. A second later I knew I was wrong, because I heard excited cries of " water, water, water," and still crying " water " the junior landed in a heap at the bottom of the ladder, having slid down the handrails at such a speed that he couldn't brake when nearing the end of the rails.

I then yelled for certain tools to be brought so that I could slacken off plugs and pipe joints on the suction side of the engine fuel pumps in order to drain off the water. Whilst frantically uncrewing plugs and nuts the engine speed was getting slower and working more and more erratically. For some reason not then apparent the starboard engine was not as yet affected and its steady beat was like music from heaven, although we knew only too well that it would resemble a noise from hades before long as both engines were supplied with fuel from the same tank. Everything was, therefore, made ready to meet such a crisis.

The engines, fortunately, were operating on gas oil, a fuel which separates much more readily from water than more viscous fuels, and the measures taken to drain off the water before it reached the engine fuel pumps were so far successful that the port engine speed increased a little. Then just as we thought that we had got rid of all the water, nothing but water filled the fuel pump suction pipes and the engine abruptly stopped. There was just time to get a little consolation from the knowledge that the starboard engine was still going well when its speed began to fall off.

Fatigue was now beginning to make itself felt, but the sound of the only remaining engine petering out gave us renewed strength, and spanners and hammers were quickly brought into use in an endeavour to get rid of the water in the pump suctions of that engine. Our efforts, however, were no more successful than they were in the case of the port engine, and soon the ship was without propulsive power and a sitting target for a Hun with a gun, providing, of course, the ship didn't sink before he could take aim.

There seemed nothing for it but to go on deck and wait for the order to abandon ship. It was heart breaking to have to give in after what had been done to save the ship that night, but I consoled myself with the thought " nothing's so bad but it might be worse," and it certainly would have been worse for me if I hadn't had my glass eye nicely tucked away in my cheek !

Before leaving the engine room I gave orders for the sea valves to be shut, as sea water was still entering the engine room through them, and with all pumps now out of action the water level was rising rapidly. It was decided to leave the dynamos to run as long as they would, as the night was very dark and the few remaining lights would help us to find our way to the lifeboats. Suddenly the two men who had been sent to shut the sea valves began shouting excitedly, and thinking they were in difficulties some of us scrambled in their direction as fast as we could in the semi-darkness. The men, who were waist-deep in water, were closing the sea valves with all speed, and as I got near enough I heard above the noise of the dynamos what they were shouting. It was " the water has stopped coming in." And sure enough it had almost stopped. In a flash I realised what had happened and scrambled back with all haste to where the other men were standing waiting for orders to leave the engine room, and shouted to them to prepare the port engine for starting. The look in their eyes clearly showed that they thought the strain of the past few hours had been too much for me.

The first requirement was to get the water out of the gravity tanks and fuel into them. The pumps, however, were under water and out of action, so the engine fuel supply pipe was disconnected near the gravity tank and buckets of fuel carried from the dynamo engine supply tank, which fortunately had remained free from water, and poured into the main engine supply pipe. The starting air compressor was also unusable, but fortunately there was sufficient compressed air in the tank for a few starts.

The port engine having been primed with water-free fuel, preparations were made to start. When all was ready the starting lever was pulled over and every man instinctively held his breath, ready either to jump over the moon or dive into the depths of despair. The first attempt was unsuccessful and the groans were pitiful to hear, but at the second attempt, just as the lever was about to be brought back to stop, the joyful sound of cylinders firing could be heard and the engine immediately gathered speed. As the engine circulating pumps were drawing water from the engine room the level soon fell sufficiently to let us get at the fuel transfer pumps, air compressors and the other essential auxiliary machines, which would enable the starboard engine to be restarted.

And so we got under way again on one engine, which was capable of giving the ship a speed of seven knots. We were off the Isle of Wight when the port engine was restarted and the journey to Newport, South Wales, where a drydock was being got ready for us, was made under Naval escort without further incident. The starboard engine was restarted during the run to Newport but had to be stopped because the efforts of all hands were required to keep the port engine going and the water in the engine room down to a level that would allow it to be worked. .

And now my technical friends can get ready to laugh. I have laughed many times since the incident, but I hope that in passing judgement they will not be too hard on me as I was only twenty-seven years old at the time, and men twice my age knew very little about diesel engines. Besides, diesel engines of that time were crude things compared with the modern product.

What actually happened was this. The torpedo had struck the ship in the cargo hold and oil bunker just forward of the engine room, situated amidships. The hole made was big enough to drive a double-decker bus through and the riveted seams in the ship's starboard side in way of the engine room had been slackened. The quantity of water entering the engine room from this cause could not have been more than 50 tons an hour. This ship, however, like all motorships of that time, was provided with a great number of overboard discharges, sea water being used for all cooling purposes, and the water which was seen pouring through the starboard side into the engine room was from these discharges which had been broken with the shock of the explosion and forced out of line. The result was that the hundreds of tons of water which should have gone overboard were being deflected back from the ship's side, and it wasn't until the starboard engine stopped that the source of in-coming water dawned upon me. That the water was slightly warmer than the sea might have been had been noticed, but this was thought to be due to some of the in-coming water making contact with the hot exhaust pipes of the main and auxiliary diesel engines.

CHAPTER IX

A CLOSE SHAVE

WHEN the *Kangaroo* put to sea again, merchant ships were still sailing independently, the convoy system not being introduced until later in the year. At the beginning of the war when the enemy was encountered on the high seas the practice was to order the crew to abandon ship, after which bombs were placed in the cargo holds and engine room by a boarding party from the submarine or surface raider. The crews were left unmolested and all they could do was to sit in lifeboats and watch their ship, and with it all their belongings, go down, and hope that some friendly ship would come along and pick them up.

Conditions were such that friendly ships could not always behave in a friendly manner. For instance, on one occasion in mid-winter after about thirty hours in a lifeboat in the Mediterranean, I and twenty-two others were overjoyed to see a large steamer coming our way. The sea was choppy, the wind cold, our thin clothes wet and the only food hard ships' biscuits, so there is no need to attempt to describe our feelings when it became only too apparent that the ship had suddenly altered course and was receding.

Many other shipwrecked mariners had similar experiences during that war, the explanation being that enemy submarines instituted the practice of launching their collapsible lifeboats as decoys and lying off within torpedo range, their hope being that one of our ships would come along, sight the lifeboat and stop to investigate. I believe they " bagged " many ships in this way until Skippers of allied ships were told to beware of such decoys.

At that time the Germans thought that by this form of warfare they would reduce the British merchant fleet so much that our people at home would soon be without food, and capitulate. They would probably have succeeded but for two factors, the first being that it takes more than an empty stomach to make a Britisher give in, and the second, the introduction of the convoy system.

When the Germans realised that the war at sea could not be won so easily, the gloves came off and the submarine warfare was " stepped-up." Merchant ships were sunk without warning and crews in open boats were allowed to get on as best they could, heedless of the state of the sea and wind or how far they were from land. In many instances the attack was so sudden and severe that there was no time to launch lifeboats, and a great many defenceless seamen perished or were maimed for life.

In spite of the war at sea being a completley one-sided affair so far as the Merchant Navy was concerned, I do not remember the sailing of a ship being delayed because a full crew could not be signed-on. There was much grumbling, but even this particular characteristic of the Britisher began to diminish when the authorities announced that owing to the adoption of unrestricted submarine warfare by the enemy, it had been decided to equip merchant ships with defensive weapons.

Convoying of merchant ships came none too soon as ships were being sunk at an alarming rate. When rescued from our lifeboats on the occasion referred to earlier, we were told by the crew of the rescuing destroyer that we were one of seven ships sunk that day. One was the P. & O. liner *Persia* with a heavy death roll. Another was a Japanese ship with not a single survivor. This was not an everyday occurrence fortunately, but sinkings were averaging twenty a week, which was much faster than the British and American shipyards could replace.

At that time the food situation at home was getting really serious. I remember going to Cardiff whilst the *Kangaroo* was repairing, and seeing long queues of women waiting in the cold outside food stores. I saw one particularly long queue outside a shop that was alleged to have potatoes. On one occasion I returned home on six days' furlough and spent much of the time looking for food. Although I had a ration card which entitled me to a meagre portion of some of the essential foodstuffs, all I was able to get before going back to sea was a small tin of condensed milk.

It took three months to repair the damaged *Kangaroo*, and when she again set out for the Middle East she was in excellent condition. Whilst repairing, a brand new 4.7″ defence gun was mounted at the after end of the ship, enclosed by a structure made of wood and canvas which collapsed instantly when so required, its purpose being to conceal the gun until it was time to use it. As this was one of the first merchant ships to be provided with defence equipment, including wireless, we were immensely proud to know that our ship was considered sufficiently important to be so equipped, and we younger ones looked forward to the time when we would make use of it, the older and wiser ones doubtless hoping that it would never be used.

However, at break of dawn on a day in April 1917 when about 180 miles South of Crete, and strangely enough in the position where I had lost a ship some two years earlier, two submarines were spotted by the look-out. The submarines were about ten miles away, and immediately the alarm was given all hands went to action stations, mine, of course, being in the engine room.

Upon sighting the submarines our ship was turned round and proceeded at maximum speed in the opposite direction. Keeping the stern of our ship to the enemy reduced the chances of being torpedoed, and put us in the best position to use our gun in the event of not being able to get away. Very soon it was apparent to those on the bridge that the submarines had the better turn of speed and began to shorten the distance between us fairly rapidly. The chase went on for about two hours before the first shot was fired by one of the submarines, and after that the firing was regular and consistent for the next half-hour or so.

At my station in the engine room I could hear the report of the enemy's guns getting louder and, on occasions, the shriek of the shells. I couldn't quite understand why we were allowing the submarines to have it all their own way when we had such a beautiful gun on board. Handing the engines over to the Second Engineer I ran up the ladders to the deck to see what was going on. At that moment the submarines would be not more than 4,000 yards astern. Visibility was such that I could see the men working the forward guns and the path of the shells could easily be followed when clear of the muzzle smoke.

It was the first time I had seen shells in flight and the sight fascinated me. I must have stood and watched some six shells make their journey, all of which dropped short or wide of our ship. The next shell to be fired came along much as the others had done, but imagine my surprise when this particular shell came straight for the ship, and before I could move or even take my eyes off the missile it crashed on the deck not more than thirty feet from me. It passed through the winch deck and penetrated the main deck, but did not pass through. By a great stroke of good luck the shell failed to explode.

If this shell had exploded the effect would, of course, have finished me, and had it entered the cargo hold where some hundreds of tons of ammunition were stored, it would have been the end of the ship, even though it failed to explode. The reason why the shell did not enter the cargo hold was that in this particular ship the deck winches were mounted on raised platforms, and the shell in passing through this platform had its velocity reduced and its force almost spent before it reached the main deck.

After this I remembered that my action station was down below, where I proceeded with haste ! Before I reached the bottom platform of the engine room I heard our gun reply, and after seven rounds firing ceased. Feeling the ship heel slightly I knew that the rudder had been put hard over, and my first thought was that the Skipper intended to turn about and ram the submarines. This, however, was not the case, the reason for the helm action being simply to evade the remaining submarine, his companion having been sunk with our seventh round. The second submarine seemed reluctant to continue the fight and we were allowed to proceed on our way.

On arriving at our destination we learned that the destroyer which had been sent to assist us in response to our wireless signals when the action began, and which did not arrive until some time after the action had terminated, reported having picked up a collapsible boat and some lifebelts, which indicated that the submarine had indeed been sunk.

CHAPTER X

MINES, NOT MINES

BY the time we had discharged our cargo and were ready to return home for another cargo the convoy system had been inaugurated. We therefore started off in the company of about ten other ships, with an auxiliary cruiser as escort. Having a stern gun, we were placed at the rear of one of the outside lines, and whilst we felt that if any ship of the company had to stop a torpedo, it would be ours, it was nevertheless comforting to be among friends.

The skippers of the ships were fully briefed by the Naval authorities before starting off, one of the essential factors being for every ship to maintain its exact position relative to the adjacent ships throughout the night as well as during the day. This, I should imagine, was far from easy in darkness, especially as all ships were running without lights. Some ships I believe got perilously near to one another but managed to avoid colliding.

After passing Gibraltar the course due West was continued until well out into the Atlantic, this with a view to avoiding enemy submarines that might be lurking off the coast of Spain. After steaming for two or three hundred miles in this direction a course due North was set.

It was whilst on this course and during a pitch black night that the silence was suddenly broken by shouts and running feet above my head, and the blowing of ships' whistles from all directions. I jumped out of my bunk and rushed on deck, to find ships all around us with lights burning, the first lights I had seen at sea since the war started. Then, before I could take in what had happened, the dim outline of a ship could be seen, making straight for us. Seconds later there came a deafening crash and our ship shuddered. She remained afloat, but our engines were so severely damaged that the voyage had to be completed on the end of a tow rope.

This accident was due to our North bound convoy meeting a

South bound convoy head-on. How many ships, if any, were sunk or how many besides ourselves damaged I cannot record, as at daybreak only the ship which had been ordered to take us in tow remained in sight.

At the end of 1917 I began to feel the strain of my war experiences and the work and worry of those early diesel engines. I was, in consequence, advised to take a light shore job for a few months. Not knowing where to look for such work I called upon my good friend Peter Youngson at South Shields Marine School to seek his advice. He gave me the name and address of a man who, he said, was looking for certificated marine engineers to do supervisory work in connection with mines. More information he couldn't give me as the telephone message had been taken by one of the girl clerks who had passed it on to him.

I called at the address the next day and after a long wait was shown into the presence of the man who required the services of certificated marine engineers. Judging by the number of files and other documents on his desk, floor and the two chairs, he was a very important man, and the brevity of the interview suggested that he was a very busy one also. However, I evidently satisfied him regarding my capabilities as I was instructed to report the following day to an address in Rotherham.

During the train journey from Newcastle to Rotherham I recalled all I had seen and learned when as a small boy I spent holidays around the coal mines in the mid-Tyne district. I presumed that the machinery in the mines around Rotherham was much the same as in the Northumberland coal mines, and that I would have no difficulty in supervising the operation and repair of winding engines and the like.

When I arrived at the address given to me I was a bit puzzled, because it was a factory, and not a coal mine as I expected. My next thought was that it was a factory where they made mining machinery and that after some training I would be sent to a coal mine in the district. After the man to whom the letter of introduction was addressed had got to know all he wanted to know about my past, he began to describe what was required of me, and as he talked very learnedly of non-magnetic metals and showed

me drawings of contrivances of which I had not the least knowledge, I became more and more bewildered. I couldn't for the life
of me think where such things could be used in a coal mine.

As the minutes passed I began to feel that a mistake had been
made. I must have been given the wrong letter of introduction.
Several times I tried to speak, but the learned man was such a fast
talker that I just couldn't get a word in edgeways. When at last
I did succeed in asking him why and where such special metals
and machines were used in coal mines, his lower jaw dropped and
his eyes opened to their fullest extent as he looked at me aghast.
When his vocal equipment would work again he said " I'm talking
about sea mines, not coal mines ! " And this was my introduction
to the magnetic mine, which for a time played havoc with our
ships some twenty-seven years later.

The magnetic mine was, therefore, a British invention, and not
of German origin as was generally supposed. The Germans were
the first to make use of this deadly weapon of war, and the reason
why the British Naval Authorities so quickly found the antidote —
degaussing — was no doubt due in a large measure to the
experimental work done during the closing stages of the 1914-18
war.

CHAPTER XI

A BLESSING IN DISGUISE

THE end of the war in November 1918 meant the end of my microscopically small contribution to the development of the magnetic sea mine. It was not until the middle of 1919, however, that I was out of a job as there was a good deal of clearing up to be done.

I had by then got used to working ashore and liked it. There were very few shore jobs going at that time, however, owing to the sudden cessation in the production of war material, so it was a case of going back to sea. Even sea berths were few and far between for the same reason, and in spite of having unique knowledge of diesel engines, the only berth offered to me was that of Fourth Engineer. This was from the employers I have now (1954) served for over thirty years, and how glad I am that I had no qualms about accepting a position so much lower in rank than I had previously held. How I very nearly missed this opportunity is perhaps worth recording as it goes to show how sometimes appearances can be deceptive.

My instructions were to join a small oil tank ship with the romantic name of *Oweenee*, at Glasgow on the following Saturday. Depositing my kit in the station left luggage office, I set off in the rain for the dock in which I expected to find my future abode. Without difficulty I found the dock, in which were two ships, neither resembling in the least an oil tanker ; besides, neither bore the name for which I was looking.

After walking the full length of the dock, I was about to return to the shipping agents, as I felt sure that my ship must be in some other dock, when a policeman appeared. In answer to my enquiry he said " Yes, you'll find her over there," pointing to a mast sticking up above the dock wall and which I had presumed belonged to a barge.

Reaching the place indicated, I looked over into the dock and there was what looked like an old sailing ship of about 3000 tons deadweight that had experienced a severe buffeting on her previous voyage. Although the cargo hatches and other deck fittings resembled those of an oil tanker, and it had a funnel at the after end which might mean that there were engines and boilers underneath, I had to walk along the dock to see if the name on the bow was the same as the one given to me.

The name was certainly the same and the port of registry was London. At first, I thought a mistake had been made and I had been sent to the wrong ship. My next thought was " what a good thing I left my heavy kit at the station." As I turned away I noticed a wooden ladder standing on the deck and reaching to within a foot of the top of the dock side. Being curious as to what kind of ship it was, I descended the ladder, and after reassuring myself that the cargo holds were intended to accommodate oil I proceeded in the direction of the funnel and to where I thought the engines, if any, might be situated.

Underneath the funnel and reaching from the deck on which I was standing to the bottom of the ship was a huge dark space, empty, as far as I could see in the fading light, except for two iron ladders and some grating, evidently intended for access to the bottom of the ship. After my eyes grew used to the dim light, I discerned what looked like two engines at the very bottom of the space. A little later I could make out the cylinder heads, and the realisation that they were diesel engines came as a surprise.

Being, of course, keenly interested in this type of engine, and not having seen one for over a year, I decided to descend to what I now knew to be the ship's engine room. At that moment a voice behind me said " Interested in diesels ? " Assuring him that I was, the owner of the voice invited me to make a closer inspection of them, an invitation I eagerly accepted. I was particularly interested when I found that they were submarine engines and was told that they were quite new. Also, that the owners were urgently in need of oil tankers to replace those sunk during the war, and as they could not wait until new tankers were built, they had hit on the idea of buying old sailing ships and installing submarine engines in them.

When we regained the deck my guide told me that the ship was to carry seven engineers and that he was Second. He went on to tell me that all hands had joined except the Fourth, and he was expected that week-end. I knew by then that no mistake had been made and that this was the ship to which I had been appointed. I straightway told the Second who I was and how he came to find me on board. He seemed pleased and I liked him, but what made me decide to go and fetch my kit was, of course, diesel engines of a type with which I had not previously sailed.

After two days on board I was promoted to Third Engineer and within a year had risen to the position of Chief. After serving a year in that capacity I was instructed to return to England. Having been away from home for two years, most of the time trading in the Red Sea, I was given a month's holiday on pay before being sent out East on my second assignment.

My destination was Singapore, and the reason for sending me there was to see if I could do anything with the machinery in a number of motor ships which had been run to a standstill. The trouble was mainly due to minor structural weaknesses in the diesel engines, and partly to those who had been in charge not knowing the peculiarities — and these were many — of this particular type of machinery.

When I reached Singapore at the end of 1921, the ships had been out of commission for a considerable time, and nothing deteriorates more quickly than a laid-up ship. Although well rusted-up the engines were more or less intact, but many of the tools and spare engine parts were missing. The ships had been in the hands of engine repairers at Singapore, Hongkong and other Eastern ports so often, that it soon became apparent that I could not expect any help from them, particularly as they need not look far to find work of a more congenial and profitable character.

As the fantastic quotations for carrying out the work in accordance with the specification I had prepared came in, my hopes of getting the ships into commission again, and being rewarded by a shore appointment, began to fade. I could not find anyone who was ready to help me. Those who were in a position to do so would listen politely and promise to speak to someone else. They never did. In fact it gradually dawned upon me that those who would not suffer in reputation had my efforts been successful, withheld their help because they felt it was throwing good money after bad.

Being determined not to admit failure until every possibility had been explored, I sought out a Chinaman who I learnt could obtain skilled as well as unskilled native labour on a commission basis. The address given to me was well inside the slum quarter of Singapore, a place I would never have visited except in desperation. Being desperate, I went forth one morning, clad in my oldest attire and without money to meet this man, who I was pleased to find was prepared to procure the labour I wanted at a price not greatly in excess of what I considered reasonable.

My scheme was to repair the machinery myself with the assistance of native labour. The engines were in most cases intact, and only required to be completely dismantled and re-built, all of which could be done on board. Each ship had a small machine shop which I hoped would make me independent of the shore establishments.

With my personal belongings, and the tools I had been able to procure from various sources, I boarded the ship I had decided to tackle first, the day before the work was to begin. She was lying at anchor about half a mile from the shore. My Chinese friend had promised to have ten Chinese fitters and twenty Malay coolies there by 7 a.m., and whilst I had no reason to doubt his word, I was greatly relieved when, after watching for about two hours, I saw some half dozen fully laden sampans (Chinese boats) leave the shore and make for the ship. Each man arrived with all his worldly possessions, which could be wrapped in a large size pocket handkerchief, the arrangement made with No. 1 Chinaman being that they should live on board, and I would provide them with their staple food, rice, and drinking water.

The first ship taken in hand was over-run with all kinds of vermin, including small black rats, which I understood were carriers of the bubonic plague, so the matter of ridding the ship of vermin, particularly the rats, had to be taken in hand without delay.

Soon after arrival in the East I acquired a small sandy-coloured mongrel dog, which I named " Tubby " because it fitted his description. He was an affectionate old thing and soon became so devoted that no matter where I went he was never more than a couple of yards from my heel, and together we often went rat-hunting. He seemed anxious enough to help, but his name described his build too accurately for him to be of much use.

The working day began at 5 a.m. on six days of the week. It was the practice of the Chinese " boy " who looked after my personal comforts so well, to put a half filled pail of water in the bath last thing each night so that it was there for me next morning should I happen to start the day at an earlier hour than usual. There was no water on board for the rats unless it rained, and they soon learnt of the practice to put water in the bathroom, but in their eagerness to get at the water, one, and sometimes two, fell into the bath, and being unable to climb the slippery sides were there next morning.

My first act each morning was to take off a slipper and kill the rat as it jumped up and slid down the side of the bath, and then throw it out of the porthole into the sea. I might have discontinued the practice of putting the pail of water in the bath and so put an end to starting each day in such an unpleasant way, but it meant one or two rats less, although the number was so great that they were doubtless increasing at a far greater rate. My native labourers also made raids on store rooms and all likely breeding places with good effect, but the number did not seem to get any less.

One day my " valet " asked for permission, which was granted, to " Go shore-side and catchee one piecee cat." Several hours later he returned exceedingly happy with an animal which he dropped at my feet. He said it was a cat, but it might have been anything. The poor thing stood where it landed and I took stock of the queerest cat I have ever seen. It was the height of an ordinary cat, but it had long thin legs, a huge head, a tail which ended in the form of a "V" and practically no torso. After looking at it long enough to convince myself that it was a cat, I remember saying " Well, there's one thing certain, and that is it will never be troubled with the belly ache because it hasn't got one."

The next morning I found a rat in the bath as usual and called out for the cat, which was quickly brought on the scene. While the rat was making frantic but unsuccessful efforts to jump out of the bath, I held the cat by the back of the neck and released my hold when I thought it would fall on the rat as it slid to the bottom of the bath. The cat sat where it landed and did not appear to notice the terrified rat scrambling from under it to continue its endeavours to jump out of the bath. In disgust I took off my slipper with the intention of carrying out the usual procedure, and with the slipper poised, it occurred to me that I might knock-out the cat first.

Whether there is such a thing as thought transmission between humans and animals I don't know, but at that instant the cat sprang as though electrified, and in no longer than it takes to wink, the cat not only caught the rat but dropped it quite dead. It all happened so suddenly that it was quite a time before I realised that I was still holding my slipper ready to strike. After getting over my surprise there came a feeling of pleasure at having found such a highly efficient ally to combat the rats, which by that time were creating some discontent amongst my labourers, and causing me much anxiety in regard to stocks of food, which in the circumstances were difficult to replace.

I went to bed that night in a much happier frame of mind, as although the cat's " bag " only numbered one, I felt sure that there would be fewer rats alive next morning. I was not, however, prepared for such slaughter. I was awakened by excited cries from the natives, and at first thought that a mutiny was well under way. I rushed out on deck to find the natives running to and fro and looking under pipes and other deck fittings, and every now and again throwing small black objects overboard. The black objects turned out to be dead rats. How many were thrown overboard before I arrived on the scene, I never found out, but the night's " bag " must have amounted to many scores. Our comical-looking cat became a favourite overnight, and not knowing the name of Dick Whittington's four-footed friend, I named our rat killer Dick, although not quite sure if it was entitled to a masculine name.

Dick cleared the ship of rats in about a couple of weeks, and although rewarded by being given good food, his shape did not alter in the least. He was so ugly that I couldn't bring myself even to stroke his head, although I often wanted to out of gratitude, but he seemed to be content with what he got, especially when Tubby showed a liking for him.

These two animals became so attached to one another that they were rarely seen more than a few yards apart, and as Tubby kept close to me it meant that the two followed me almost everywhere. The only part of the ship they would not venture into was the engine room, because of the widely spaced bars in the grating, but would lay side by side on the grating inside the door until I returned.

When I had occasion to go ashore, Tubby always went too. He could negotiate gangways and clamber into small boats when the ship was anchored in the bay, better than any sailor. On such occasions the cat would go almost frantic at being left behind and run backwards and forwards along the deck crying pitifully. At first it made no attempt to follow Tubby down the gangway, for fear, I suppose, of falling into the water. When Tubby returned he was always given the warmest reception. It was indeed good to see such affection in animals and not a little surprising considering the cat was almost in a wild state when it was brought on board.

Then one day the cat cautiously followed the dog down the gangway and jumped into the sampan waiting to take me ashore. Not wanting the cat ashore, I and the Chinese boatman tried to catch it, but it became so ferocious that we gave up the attempt. I therefore had to do my business in Singapore and have my lunch that day in the customary hotel with Tubby and this queer looking creature, which attracted more attention than I liked, never more than a few feet away from me.

That was only the beginning. The cat soon became adept at getting off ships and into boats, and the only way I could stop the cat was to leave Tubby behind when I went ashore. I did this once but couldn't bear to see the pathetic look in his eyes the second time. I therefore had to get used to the jibes of Europeans and the embarrassing amusement of the natives.

CHAPTER XII

MY TIME IN SAIL

DURING my two years in the East I had the rare distinction of serving for a few months as Chief Engineer of a fully rigged 3000 ton deadweight sailing ship. She was about forty-five years old, and probably one of the last to be made of wrought iron, as against mild steel used at the present time.

The *Dolphinshell* had made some good passages in her time and it seemed all wrong to fit her with a propeller driven by oil engines so near the end of her successful life. The masts and sails, however, were, I am pleased to say, retained ; the hot-bulb type engines being used only when entering and leaving harbour or when becalmed at sea, when the engines were capable of giving the ship a speed of four knots only.

Never did a ship's Chief Engineer have so little responsibility or such an easy job. The power of the engines was so small in relation to the size of ship that with a fair wind the ship, which was capable of spanking along at twelve knots under sail alone, would begin driving the engines through the propeller ! When this happened, the ignition bulbs of the engine cooled down and it was impossible to keep the engine working, even if there had been any advantage in doing so. In these circumstances the only thing to do was to declutch the engine and become a passenger until the wind changed.

Although the engines had long periods of idleness, parts wore out, and the engine had of course to be maintained in good order. It was occasionally necessary, therefore, to order spare parts through the Owners' Head Office in London. Instead of getting the parts, along would come a letter saying they couldn't understand why engine parts were required for a full rigged sailing ship, and when the Skipper indented for canvas and sail tackle he invariably received a letter asking why he wanted such things when the ship was mechanically propelled.

Had the writers of those letters been with us when, driven

solely by engine power we rounded a point against the tide, they would have got different ideas about mechanical propulsion, especially with engines of such low power and type. More than once during the few months I was in the ship, did we sight a beacon early in the morning, and it was still there when darkness fell, even though the engines had behaved themselves and run continuously throughout the day at maximum power.

The Skipper, Captain Barber, had been in the ship ever since she was built, except for occasional short periods. He was a real old salt, and a most genial man with a passion for animals. His liking was not for any particular kind, for when I joined the ship there were monkeys, dogs, cats, parrots, goats and even a young bear on board.

The monkeys had full scope for their extreme agility in the ship's rigging, and their antics caused much amusement. Some of them were quite wild and savage while others were very tame. Although the wild ones never came down to the deck except for food and water, and then only if nobody happened to be about, they showed no desire to leave the ship, even when in ports where the chatter and shrieks of their kinsmen in the near-by trees could be distinctly heard.

While pacing backwards and forwards along the short deck one fine afternoon, I saw something go over the side into the sea. I didn't think much about the incident until I saw a second article disappear overboard. Being then a bit curious, I extended my walk a little further so that I could see who it was throwing things away. As I approached the spot one of our wild monkeys came into view, carrying a large framed photograph which it had taken from the apprentices' cabin, the door having been left open as is customary in the tropics. I ran forward to retrieve the picture, and although the monkey reached the ship's side before me, my prompt intervention spoilt his aim and it fell on the deck. The monkey retreated, but evidently not far enough, because when I bent down to pick up the picture I received a vicious bite on my posterior !

I never saw such big cockroaches as lived on board that ship. There were thousands of them and some were quite two inches long. The really big ones never ventured into the open except at night, and then only if all lights were out. At certain times, when breeding I was told, they would fly. This generally occurred, much to our annoyance, after we had " turned-in " for the night and put out the light. The noise made by their wings and the force with which they struck the wooden bulkheads was enough to awaken the soundest sleeper. I generally kept a slipper handy and when the noise got too bad would switch on the light in the hope of killing a few. They were, however, much too quick for me, and although I must have switched on the light for the purpose hundreds of times, I never really had more than a fleeting glimpse of them as they disappeared like a flash through openings in the woodwork or into drawers or cupboards.

I visited Susu in Sumatra on two occasions. At that time Susu was merely a clearing on the edge of a forest which extended down to the sea. The forest had also been cleared a few miles inland to enable an oil well to be drilled, the crude oil being pumped through pipes to a big circular tank at Susu. Apart from half-a-dozen white men, the population comprised about 200 natives who lived in ramshackle huts made of anything upon which they could lay their hands.

One of the difficulties experienced by the hardy oil pioneers in those parts was the prevalence of malaria, due to the presence of myriads of mosquitos. To attack these pests at their breeding grounds by pouring paraffin on the swamps was a hopeless task, and if some other means had not been found it is doubtful if the work could have proceeded.

It sometimes happened that the first well drilled produced nothing but highly inflammable petroleum gas, which was ejected skywards with great force. Not being of any particular value at that time the gas was ignited and burnt continuously like a gigantic torch, the flame sometimes extending upwards for fully one hundred feet. At night the long, thin, smokeless flame could be seen several miles away, and the reflected light for many times that distance. This in itself was a grand sight, but as darkness fell, what appeared at first to be a haze and then a thin cloud would gather and drift towards the flame, where it quickly dispersed.

The drifting cloud was not smoke, however, but literally millions and millions of moths and mosquitos attracted from near and far by the flame, in which they perished.

Cocoanut trees abounded in and around Susu, and during my first visit I met a man of doubtful nationality who made a living gathering and exporting not only the nuts, but the coir fibre which grows around them. The tall straight trunks of these branchless trees were alive with red ants, which made it very unpleasant for men to climb them. The difficulty was overcome in this instance by a female orang-outang named Daisy, trained when young to climb the trees and throw the cocoanuts to the ground.

Daisy was, at the time of my visit to Susu, a wise old ape and could be very amusing. My first meeting with her and her master was on a Sunday morning. Being a day of rest, I and some others were idling on deck when our attention was called to the comical pair coming on board. Although it was apparant that one was a man and the other a beast they had much in common. Both were about the same height and build, and whilst Daisy was covered with long red-brown hair, her master wore a suit much too big for him of a similar colour. They had the same slow ambling gait and exhibited the same curiosity towards the things they passed as they came slowly along the deck towards us, the man starting conversation by a " Good morning, gentlemen."

The man had local knowledge which interested us so much that nobody noticed that Daisy had left the group and wandered off, until she was seen emerging from the Second Mate's cabin dressed in that worthy's uniform jacket. After much fun at the Second's expense, the garment was taken from Daisy and returned to its rightful owner, probably with many of the things which kept Daisy constantly scratching.

When in port it was the custom on Sundays, for the ship's officers to assemble about 11 a.m. in the saloon for a glass of iced beer. On this occasion Daisy's master was invited to join us. Whilst we were sitting around the saloon table having our cool drink and listening to the experiences of our guest, Daisy ambled in and sat in one of the vacant chairs. She made it very apparent that she too wanted a drink. When asked what should be given to her, her master suggested a glass of iced water, knowing no doubt what the result would be. When it was handed to her Daisy put the glass to her nose, turned her head away from us and handed it back to the giver with such a humanly disdainful look on her face that caused roars of laughter. Beer was then brought, and never did I see a glass of beer disappear so quickly.

On our second visit to Susu some four weeks later, we were told that both Daisy and her master were dead. It happened this way. One day soon after our first visit the pair set out for a normal day's work, Daisy to climb the trees and her master to gather the cocoanuts she threw down. Daisy apparently was not inclined to work that day, and her master beat her. She then began working, but when moving on to the next tree she came up behind her master, placed her open hands on each side of his head and with a sudden jerk broke his neck. Death, we were told, by those with knowledge of this kind of beast, would be instantaneous. Daisy stood over her victim and would not allow anybody to go near. She therefore had to be shot.

The ferocious nature of this particular type of ape was described by a big-game hunter when some time afterwards the Skipper was asked to take a baby orang-outang to Manilla. He said they never leave their young unguarded. The female remains constantly with its off-spring until it is old enough to take care of itself, and the male absents himself only long enough to get food for his family. The orang-outang is tremendously strong and agile, and to capture a young specimen it is generally necessary to keep observation at a safe distance, sometimes for days, until both parents can be shot at the same time. Our hunter friend said that if one only was killed the other seemed to sense the direction from which the fatal bullet came, and woe betide the hunter if he is not quick with his gun.

The baby orang-outang we were asked to take to Manilla could not have been more than a few months old and was as ugly as it is possible to imagine any living thing. When any of the other monkeys on board went near, it would let off howls which could be heard in any part of the ship, but it was surprisingly quiet and

In a flash Jacko swung his body round and caught hold of Ginger with one of his feet.

content when in human society.

Being sorry for the little creature, which was given the name Ginger, I gave it some attention. This was evidently to its liking because whenever it saw me at a distance it would cry pitifully until I went to it. Although so young, it would take hold of two of my fingers in such a vice-like grip that a good deal of effort was required to free them. It enjoyed being swung round and round at arm's length and the faster one went the better it liked it. Before very long it became customary to take my daily walking exercise on deck with Ginger happily swinging from the fingers of one hand, its free hand pressed on the top of its head.

Prior to Ginger coming on board I used to make a little fuss of another monkey named Jacko. He was a friendly little chap, no bigger than a cat, with a coat of fine grey fur. His movements were as quick as lightning and when in the mood he could be very mischievous. By monkey standards he was considered intelligent, and was by far the most popular animal on board.

Jacko evidently had a jealous streak in his nature too, since he resented the attention given to Ginger. He didn't hurt Ginger, but never missed an opportunity to grasp him by an arm or leg and drag him along the deck, poor Ginger howling as though he were being killed by inches. It got so bad that Jacko had to be chained, as it was necessary for health reasons to let Ginger have his freedom. Judging by the miserable expression on Jacko's face, no worse form of punishment could have been inflicted.

Whether Ginger got pleasure from seeing Jacko chained I don't know, but he would sometimes approach Jacko and sit just out of reach, calmly watching him frantically springing to the limit of his chain in an endeavour to get at his unwanted shipmate.

On one occasion Jacko sat as far out as his chain would allow. He was unusually quiet, with a decided look of repentance in his eyes, watching Ginger who sat facing him. The look on his face and the subdued noises in his throat could easily have been interpreted as a plea for closer relations. This was apparently Ginger's interpretation, because every few minutes he would wriggle a few inches nearer to Jacko.

The last move brought Ginger within about eighteen inches of

Jacko, who instantly became electrified and in a flash had swung his body round and caught hold of Ginger's arm with one of his feet. In a moment the scene was transformed from peace to war. The jubilant shrieks from Jacko and the howls of distress from Ginger could have been heard miles away. Fortunately I took in the situation in time to grab Jacko by the back of the neck and separate them before his teeth got too far into the fleshy part of Ginger.

For some time after this incident Jacko was in disgrace, and my punishment was to take less notice of him. He was fully aware of this, since whenever I passed without giving him the usual rub under the chin, his sorrowful eyes would follow me as I walked along the deck.

Jacko was not completely remorseful, however, because on one occasion I chanced to turn round and look in his direction, whereupon he pushed forward his head and pulled a face at me. When I pretended to retrace my steps to administer just punishment the sorrowful look again came into his eyes, and with head bent and hands together he began playing with his fingers. These antics were repeated every time I turned round, until in the end he was forgiven and our normal friendly relationship resumed.

CHAPTER XIII

A REALLY TOUGH JOB

WHEN my work in the East had been completed a message was received from my Chief in London instructing me to return home immediately. I left Singapore by ship within a week. At that time (1923) there was not, of course, any passenger aeroplane service.

After being cordially greeted at the London office, my immediate superior informed me that I was required to take over the engine department of a recently acquired ship named the *Trigonia*, then at a West Coast port. Further, that as the ship had been waiting five days for me I was to proceed direct, even though I had been abroad for almost two years. However, my Chief relented somewhat before I started off and allowed me to spend twenty-four hours at my home, then at Whitley Bay, before proceeding to Barrow-in-Furness.

The *Trigonia* was a 10,000 ton deadweight oil tanker, built for the Admiralty during the early part of the first world war and for seven years had an inglorious career under four names. As the ship did not change owners each time her name was changed, the assumption is that this was done in the hope that it would change her luck and result in less trouble with the two 8-cylinder open fronted 1500 H.P. diesel propelling engines, which were complicated, cumbersome and crude when compared with present-day products.

From being commissioned until I made her acquaintance, most of the *Trigonia's* life had been spent in various foreign ports throughout the world undergoing alterations and repairs, or waiting for new engine parts to be sent from home. The troubles experienced were so serious that one of the Chief Engineers found the strain too much and the poor chap committed suicide, while to escape the hard, unhealthy work, many of the ratings broke their agreements and deserted.

When in the London office, I was told in all good faith that the ship had been eight weeks at Barrow repairing and was then ready for sea. Instead of the ship being ready to cast off her mooring ropes as soon as I went aboard, I found a situation which almost beggars description. The engine room and the scores of men working on the engines were indescribably dirty, bits of machinery, tools, ropes, lifting tackle, etc. were lying all over the place, the air in the engine room was so thick with smoke and oil vapour that it made the eyes smart, and the noise made by the auxiliary machinery and the men shouting to one another was deafening.

All repairs considered necessary by the Superintendent-in-Charge had, it is true, been completed, and endeavours, started several days before, were being made to get the engines to operate preparatory to sailing. Starting was a very uncertain affair, and when the engine did start on compressed air it was questionable if it would operate on fuel when the lever was put over to the corresponding position. From the cylinders that did " fire," smoke and sparks would belch forth as though the fitting of piston rings had been overlooked.

The reversing gear of both engines was in such a bad condition that when an engine did start with the reversing gear in the ahead position, there was no certainty that it would run in that direction, and when it elected to run in the reverse direction the engine would draw air through the exhaust valves and discharge the burning gases through the air inlet valves into the engine room, filling it with smoke, blinding and choking everybody.

The custom of advising the men working above the cylinder head level when an engine was about to be started was a wise precaution, because when it began operating in the direction opposite from that intended, large pieces of metal from the slotted air inlet pipes would fly in all directions. It was, nevertheless, rather funny to see all hands in the upper part of the engine room quickly drop and lie face downwards when the warning shout " look out we're starting " was heard.

This particular make of engine was quite new to me, so that it was not until the second or third day on board that I was able to assess what I was up against as Chief Engineer. Even after two months of strenuous effort on the part of a whole army of fitters and other trades, the engines were in a deplorable condition, but whether the cause was bad design or wanton neglect, I was not then in a position to judge. About one thing there was not the slightest doubt. It was that whilst I had in the past come up against some tough diesel engines, those in the *Trigonia* were going to prove the toughest of all.

To make matters worse, the Superintendent-in-Charge, a little man with big ideas, one of which was about his own abilities, was quite incapable of handling such a difficult situation. His experience of those early diesel engines was very limited and his knowledge of their peculiarities was even more so. Add to this his blank refusal to listen to suggestions, or even to discuss the probable causes of the difficulties encountered, and you will get a vague idea of the unsatisfactory state of affairs. It was plain to everyone except the little man that unless the defective parts so far overlooked were put right, no progress would be made, and the ship would never leave port under her own power. His often repeated remark was " I will get these engines to run even if it is the last thing I do." It so happened that it was the last thing he did for his employers at that time.

Although I was rather disgruntled at having been brought home so hurriedly and not allowed more time with my family after such a long absence, the job interested me and I was eager to see what I could do to put matters right, particularly as I had been told that my reward for doing so would be promotion to Superintendent Engineer.

I therefore approached the Skipper of the ship, a fine old chap, with the suggestion that he should accept the ship and proceed with tugs to a safe anchorage where I would have a free hand and we, the ship's engineers, could get down to things ourselves. Although the engines were incapable of operating one hour continuously the Superintendent, to my surprise and joy, readily agreed to the proposal. The ship was accordingly towed to a safe anchorage some thirty miles distant.

On arrival at the anchorage, all engine room hands were told to rest for six hours and then begin watches of eight hours on and

Scores of men working on the engines.

six off. During the six hours that the engineers and ratings were getting some well earned sleep, I made a thorough examination of the engines and decided that the starting mechanism would first of all require to be put in order. Then, when this part was in such a condition that the engine would start with certainty, the reason for it failing to begin working on fuel in the desired direction would next have to be discovered and the fault remedied.

For seven days the work continued without interruption, not even pausing at the change of watches. Those eleven engineers and eight ratings worked as few men worked before or since under really heart-breaking conditions, and for a Chief Engineer who was practically unknown to them. More good work could have been done, but I didn't want to delay the ship too long and, moreover, it was beyond human endurance for men to work much longer at such a rate. We had in those seven days put the two engines into a condition which would ensure them starting and running in the direction intended with certainty.

After all hands had rested for twelve hours, preparations were made to begin the voyage to Tampico in Mexico. A few hours after leaving the anchorage the atmosphere in the engine room became so thick owing to leakage of dense obnoxious gas past the sixteen pistons, that it was quite impossible to see further than a couple of yards, whilst what with the roar of the escaping gases and the noise made by the valve gear, conversation was possible only by placing one's mouth within an inch of the other's ear.

Every now and again sheets of flame would shoot out from the bottoms of the cylinders, so that I did not think it prudent to remove the fire hose which had been laid along the middle grating by the fitters before they went ashore. The purpose of the hose was apparently to extinguish fires, caused by the greasy matter which rapidly accumulated under the cylinders being set alight by the flame passing the pistons.

We hadn't been under way very long before there was reason to use the fire hose, and when it is remembered that the engines were of the open fronted type and that much of the sea water from the hose consequently passed into the crankcase and mixed with the bearing lubricating oil, the effect upon the bearings can be better imagined than described. To avoid having to use the hose, the accumulated oily matter had to be periodically removed by shovelling it into buckets, as this was the only way to prevent fires.

During the run across the Atlantic the engines stopped, or had to be stopped, thirty-two times. Sometimes matters could be put right in minutes, but generally it took hours of hard slogging. For part of the time the work was made more arduous by the ship pitching and rolling in a seaway, and dangerous because of the difficulty in keeping one's feet on gratings and platforms made slippery by the oil-laden atmosphere of the engine room.

We arrived at Tampico twenty-six days after leaving home waters. Had the engines been in good shape the voyage would have taken sixteen days. Although few ships must have crossed the Atlantic with greater difficulty, even in the early days of steam ships, the engines were in better condition at the end of the voyage as a result of the hard work done by the grand team of men I was fortunate in having on my staff. There was, of course, much more still to be done.

One of the first jobs tackled at sea was to make the cylinder relief valves serviceable, since when the ship left all such valves were jammed hard on their seats by wooden wedges and would not function at any cylinder pressure. This extraordinary and highly dangerous method of overcoming one trouble was thought necessary, because whenever excessive pressure occurred in the cylinders and the valves lifted, the heat of the escaping gases softened the springs and made them collapse. It is no wonder, therefore, that cylinder heads and pistons were broken and other parts of the engine seriously strained when, owing to the neglected condition of the fuel pumps, excessive quantities of fuel were injected into the cylinders.

The cause of the springs collapsing was found to be their location, which was near the point where the high temperature gases left the cylinders, and all that was required to put matters right was to alter the position of the internal parts in such a way that the springs were transferred to the upper part of the valve. Once the cause had been discovered the remedy was soon effected.

The state of the engine room was so bad that it is not now easy to believe that the human frame could endure such conditions. As an illustration, the Skipper, who made a practice of visiting me every morning before breakfast to enquire how things had been going during the night, began on one occasion by saying " The job seems to be going better this morning Chief." It so happened that we had had a busy night but at that moment both engines were running and we were waiting for the next thing to happen. I asked what made him think things were different from any other morning, and he said " There's more smoke coming out of the funnel (from two boilers) than out of the skylights, so I thought things must be better down below."

On another occasion when manoeuvring the ship either in or out of port, I forget which, I mounted the starting platform and observed that one engine was running in the opposite direction from that shown on the engine room telegraph. I immediately stopped the engine and then started it in the right direction. When the Third Engineer, who was operating the engine, was reprimanded he petulantly replied " Why don't you put the telegraph where a fellow can see it ? " The position of the telegraph at that time was only about three feet from the eye of the operator, the trouble being that it could not be clearly seen through the smoke-laden air. In order that such a serious mistake would not be made again, I promptly picked up a spanner, and after breaking the glass in the face of the telegraph turned to the Third and said, " If you can't see the pointer you can feel it and there will be no excuse in future for starting in the wrong direction."

The foul atmosphere was, of course, due to dense smoke blowing past the sixteen main engine pistons. When an opportunity occurred to investigate this excessive blow past, it was found that although the fuel injection valves were set, and rightly, with the engine at rest to open at 5 degrees before top centre, the movement in the gear operating the valves when the engine was working was so great that injection did not take place until well after top centre. This, it was realised, could be the cause of many of our troubles, among which might be failure of the engine to pick up promptly on fuel, high fuel consumption, low power output, excessive heat in pistons, cylinder covers cracking, destruction of lubricating oil film on cylinder walls, etc., etc.

When the weather was good enough the ship was stopped and a start made to advance the timing. The maximum possible adjustment of the operating gear was found to be wholly insufficient, and the camshafts had to be lifted and rotated relative to the crankshaft by one or two teeth at a time. Although the ship was rolling about, this heavy job was undertaken with good heart, because as each alteration was made an improvement was apparent. When the camshafts were in the position which resulted in the least amount of blow past the pistons, a check on the timing was made and this was found to be about 50 degrees before top centre when the engine was at rest. No wonder the engines wouldn't develop anything like full power and filled the engine room with smoke and oily vapour !

Although improvements resulted from this alteration, the pistons were still blowing more than they should, and as this was now thought to be due to the piston rings being jammed in their grooves, it was decided to remove all pistons and free them. As, however, most of the engineers had been working continuously for about twenty hours, it was considered wise to delay this further heavy task until next day.

In the interval I kept a close watch on the engines and was pleased to observe a considerable improvement, so much in fact that although my hands were swollen with continuous handling of tools, and my arms and legs, not to mention my back, aching as a result of swinging heavy hammers and hauling on chain lifting tackle, I was itching to get those piston rings freed. I lay down on the floor of my cabin but couln't sleep, and after a while took over below so that the watch-keeping engineer could get some sleep and be refreshed for the heavy work ahead.

The port engine was accordingly stopped after breakfast next morning, and breakdown watches of eight hours on and four off arranged. After the eight pistons of the port engine had been dealt with and the engine re-started, the starboard engine was stopped. The weather was not too good and the rolling of the ship made it difficult to keep one's balance, but we were thankful for a moderately strong wind which cleared the engine room of some of the foul gas. Everything was covered with a black, slimy mixture of carbon and oil, but in spite of the difficulty of holding slippery tools and skating about on the grease covered gratings, the whole job was completed in under sixty hours. How those men worked! When the last nut was hardened up and the engine re-started they just flopped where they stood and were almost too tired to begin wiping the slime from their bodies.

After a well-earned rest, a start was made to get rid of some of the dirt and grease which covered the whole engine room and everything in it, and as the blow past the pistons had been almost stopped, we began to wear normal engine room clothing. Ordinary boiler suits and the like, by the way, had been found to be quite out of the question as they soon became covered with grease and could not be cleaned. It was, therefore, the practice to cover our bodies with sacks in which three holes were cut in the closed end, one for the head and two for the arms.

Whilst this alteration to the timing of the fuel valves and freeing of the piston rings had resulted in a great improvement in the condition of the engine room, we still had many other troubles to overcome, one of which was breaking of crankpin bearing bolts. Though the engine could generally be stopped before both bearing bolts had broken, on two occasions this was not possible.

On the first of these two occasions we had spent some twenty-eight hours changing cracked pistons and carrying out other repairs, after which the engine was again started up. Whilst on deck having a breath of fresh air before beginning to remove the dirt from my person, I heard and felt a heavy thump. After listening for a moment I realised that the speed of one engine had been reduced. Going down below I asked the Fourth Engineer, who was standing at the controls, what had happened. He shook his head, indicating that he did not know.

Everything seemed to be in order excepting that one engine was running slightly slower than the other. The fuel and other gauges which might indicate the cause of the engine running slow were registering correctly, and then I noticed that no pressure was showing on the port engine lubricating oil gauge. I immediately stopped that engine and began looking round to see where the oil was going, expecting to find that the pump had stopped or that one of the oil pipes at the back of the engine had broken.

When I reached the back of the engine I saw a large gaping hole opposite No. 4 crank and thick black oil dripping from everything in the vicinity. Peering into the crankcase I failed to see the connecting rod in the dim light, so went and brought a lamp. Sure enough, the connecting rod had gone. Turning my head in the direction of the ship's side, there was the piston, piston rod and connecting rod still connected together, standing up against the ship's side as though it had been put there by block and tackle. To reach this position the parts had been thrown for a distance of twelve feet and had passed between two auxiliary machines which were spaced only fifteen inches apart. That such large and heavy parts were thrown between them with such force and without doing additional damage is hard to believe.

What had happened was that one four-and-a-half inch diameter crankpin bolt had broken and the second bolt had broken immediately afterwards. The revolving crank caught the foot of the connecting rod and flung the three connected parts, weighing a total of about $2\frac{1}{2}$ tons, against the ship's side.

A start was made to strengthen the bedplate and columns with angle bars, plates, stay bolts, etc., and as most of the strengthening members had to be cut from the rough it was another thirty hours before that engine was again set in motion, with No. 4 running gear still leaning against the ship's side.

The exhaust valves, also, were very troublesome, and until this fault could be remedied it was wise not to stop the engines when near land unless it was really necessary. When the engines stopped, the water-cooled steel exhaust valve spindles generally jammed owing to unequal contraction of certain parts, and they had to be worked free by spanners and crowbars before the engine could be started again in either direction, an operation that generally took fifteen minutes. Sometimes the parts became so tightly jammed that the whole valve had to be replaced by another, and this couldn't be done under half an hour.

Such was the state of affairs with this particular part of the engine on a voyage to a place called Fall River in the U.S.A. After discharging cargo we had to pass through a swing bridge in order to reach the open sea. When rounding a bend in the river which brought the bridge within view, the bridge was seen to be closed. Not wishing to stop the engines for the reasons just given, the Skipper blew the ship's whistle vigorously and in good time.

The bridge attendants were either having a quiet game of cards or resented being given such an early and insistent warning of our approach. In any event, the bridge remained closed and it was apparent that it would not open until it pleased the attendants, who of course would be quite ignorant of the engine difficulties likely to result from their inattention to duty.

When there was no sign of the bridge opening the Skipper got anxious, and kept telegraphing the engine room for less and still less speed. This involved difficulties, because the engines at that time might stop if run too slowly, due to the poor condition of the valve gear. By this time the ship was getting dangerously near to the bridge, and in the end the engines had to be stopped to prevent a collision. The result was, of course, that many of the exhaust valves jammed, and the ship was carried along on the tide towards the still closed bridge.

The Skipper took the only course open to him and the first anchor was " let go." The ship swung round a half turn but the anchor failed to hold her against the tide, so she continued stern first towards the bridge, dragging the anchor after her. The second anchor was then " let go," without having the desired effect. The ship was now within about a hundred yards of the bridge and only the bridge attendants could prevent a serious accident.

When the bridge attendants realised that we were unable to use our engines, and that their bridge was in danger of being smashed to pieces, they opened the bridge in what must have been record time. The opening was completed not a moment too soon, for the stern of the ship was already between the piers. The old ship continued on her way stern first, dragging both anchors, and, believe it or not, she passed between the bridge structures without touching anything. When the other side of the bridge was

reached the anchors took hold and the ship came quietly to rest.
Twenty minutes later the engines were in working order and we
made for the open sea without hearing what the bridge attendants
had to say about us.

My last voyage in the *Trigonia* was made eleven months after
joining. The run from Tampico to Genoa, a distance of 5,755
miles, being made non-stop. Before arrival at our destination the
engine room had been scraped, washed down with paraffin, and
given its first coat of paint for many a long day.

CHAPTER XIV

NECESSITY THE MOTHER OF INVENTION

ONE of my first jobs after leaving the sea was to stand-by the construction, and afterwards the testing, of a double-acting diesel engine. The engine was built at Wallsend-on-Tyne, and in order to give some idea of its size, I would mention that the six-throw crankshaft weighed 73 tons and the whole engine 600 tons, while the horse-power developed in its six 30-inch diameter cylinders was 4400. Being the first engine of its kind there were many problems to be solved.

When the time arrived to test the engine, one of the troubles experienced was breaking of the pipes in the piston rods used to convey the cooling water to the fast moving pistons. The pipes, which were about 10 feet long and 2 inches diameter were made of bronze, and it soon became evident that a tougher material, such as steel, was necessary. The steel pipes substituted were tough enough to withstand the stresses, but this material was found to corrode rapidly. Attention was therefore given to finding a tough material which would resist the corrosive elements in the water passing through the pipes.

Stainless steel pipes were procured, but a short time in use proved that the claim of non-corrodibility of such materials was either exaggerated or that the conditions in this particular engine were unusually severe. To fit new pipes in the six piston rods entailed a dozen men working night and day for a week, so that apart from the time lost, the cost to change these pipes was considerable.

After three different brands of stainless steel pipes had been fitted and failed, I turned my mind towards making an apparatus which would subject samples of materials submitted by the steel makers to the conditions prevailing in the engine, and so eliminate the time and cost of making and fitting pipes which might prove no better than those previously tried.

The corrosive conditions were thought to be brought about by combination of hot, highly aerated water, which due to the rapid reciprocating motion of the pistons was kept in a state of great turbulence, and excessive stress in the material. The apparatus, which was constructed mainly from odd bits of material taken from the works' scrap heap, presented a very " Heath Robinson " appearance, but conditions closely approaching those in the engine were procured. Consequently, as the samples of material considered likely to withstand the corrosive elements came forward, they were tested in the apparatus. When microscopically examined, many of the samples showed signs of corroding after only a short time and none was considered good enough for the job.

At one stage so many samples had been rejected that it seemed as though a suitable material was not available, and the statement that there was no such material as *stainless* steel justified. This rather bold statement was made by my Chief in London, and when it reached the heart of the steel making industry, namely Sheffield, it, as can be imagined, created quite a stir. The result was that samples of steel under names and numbers of which we had never heard before, were sent forward, but without exception they were unable to withstand completely the conditions set up in the test apparatus.

All concerned were beginning to get very anxious, because the engine which had cost about £100,000 would be useless without these particular pipes, and even the designers of the engine didn't seem able to re-design this part so that not-so-strong but corrosive resistant material, such as bronze, could be used. All agreed that the pipes would have to be made of steel, but no two agreed upon how they were to be made non-corrosive. All sorts of suggestions were made and some, such as galvanising and chrome plating mild steel pipes, were tried but without success.

One of the leading metallurgists of that time was the late Dr. Hadfield, who, when the samples which had been sent to Wallsend for testing were returned showing unmistakable signs of corrosion, requested that the test apparatus should be sent to Sheffield. The whole outfit could be easily carried, so there was no difficulty in complying promptly with such a request. When the apparatus was produced on arrival at Sheffield the experts were, quite naturally, inclined to be cynical. However, they had ready many samples of special steels which, I was informed, had been subjected to, and successfully withstood, all recognised tests. Nevertheless, after a few days' testing there was not one of those samples which did not show signs of corroding after exposure in my crude apparatus.

Among the experts who personally witnessed the testing, Dr. Hadfield was outstanding, not only because of his vast knowledge of these special steels, but his admission that they had been found wanting and that, in the light of these tests, the statement that stainless steel had yet to be discovered was justified. For the next week I had the good fortune to be associated with Dr. Hadfield and his work, and whilst at the end of the week the desired product had not been produced, there were indications that if there was such a thing as completely non-corrodible steel, he was the man who would dicover it.

Soon after I parted from Dr. Hadfield, he retired to his laboratory, where I learned afterwards he worked, ate and slept for three weeks. At the end of that time I was asked to return to Sheffield with my apparatus in order to test out a new material. I accordingly journeyed to Sheffield, and on arrival found Dr. Hadfield in an optimistic mood. The small sample of material which he produced was about one inch long and half-an-inch in diameter and very highly polished. No time was lost in testing this sample, and after half-an-hour it was removed and a microscopic examination did not reveal any indication of corrosion. The sample was returned to the apparatus and allowed to remain for an hour, making a total time of one-and-a-half hours. The sample was again microscopically examined and found to be still unaffected in the least degree.

In comparison with the samples previously tested, it was evident that something really good had been discovered, and the test was continued until the sample had been subjected to the drastic conditions produced in the apparatus for twelve hours. The twelve hours came to an end at three o'clock one morning, and when the sample was removed and eagerly examined, I remarked that not only was there no sign of corrosion, but that the sample " stays bright."

It was then decided to return the sample to the apparatus for a further twelve hours, since whilst no other sample had proved completely resistant for twelve hours, this further test would confirm or refute the conclusions already reached.

Dr. Hadfield and I then left the laboratory. We returned after breakfast and remained there, doing nothing but talk, smoke and watch, until the sample was taken out of the apparatus in its original bright condition.

This test took place thirty years ago, and since then that piece of non-corrodible steel has, except for short periods, lain in the water spout of the garage at my home, and even now when rubbed between the fingers its original brightness is revealed. Moreover, there are a great many engineers who will agree with me that nothing better than this particular brand of steel, which has become so widely known, has so far been produced.

We were, of course, overjoyed at the success of Dr. Hadfield's good work, and he naturally was in high spirits when he saw me off at the railway station. We talked until the train was about to move, when it suddenly occurred to him that he would like me to have the first article to be made from this absolutely non-corrodible steel. As the train was moving I had very little time to think, but as we gathered speed I shouted, " Make me a pie dish". That, as I have already said, was about thirty years ago, and that pie dish, after regular use, is still in service and is as bright now as the day it was made.

A few days after my return home I received a letter saying that Dr. Hadfield intended to throw a small private party in celebration of the discovery and inviting me to attend. It was a very pleasant function, and when Dr. Hadfield was asked what name he intended to give to the wonderful material which had been made to his formula, he replied that he could think of none better than a combination of the two words which had been spoken when we examined the sample after the first twelve hour test, and the two words were " stays bright." Subsequently the words were combined and became " Staybrite."

The importance of this discovery will be appreciated when it is remembered that the estimated quanity of steel lost every year by corrosion is forty million tons. In addition, a colossal quantity of paint is used, otherwise the wastage of steel would be much greater. If, therefore, all steel used was of " Staybrite " quality the benefits to mankind would be great indeed, as the saving effected would ultimately be beneficially reflected in the standard of living.

When " Staybrite " steel was first produced it had certain disadvantages from a constructional point of view. Firstly, it was difficult to machine, and although special cutting tools were employed, the cost to fashion it made its use uneconomical except in special cases. Also, the cost to produce was very much greater than that of ordinary steel. The cost is still higher than that of other steels, but if it will last for ever it will, for many applications, be the cheapest in the end.

Steel plays such an important part in our present civilization that anything that can be done to preserve it will be of immense benefit to mankind. No other material is used in anything like such quantity, and yet no other material wastes away so rapidly. It is not surprising, therefore, that much money and effort is being expended in an endeavour to find a means of preserving this very essential material, but the ideal solution is, of course, the production of a steel such as " Staybrite " at a price which would be economic for general purposes.

CHAPTER XV

ALL IN A DAY'S WORK

IN the early 1920's, soon after I became an assistant Superintendent Engineer, my employers placed orders for the construction of twelve 10,000 ton deadweight ships, to be propelled by double-acting diesel engines of an entirely new and untried design. Some said that the step was progressive but rather bold, whilst others, at a later date, said it was a very unwise one. Subsequent events proved the latter view to be correct, but then it is easy to be wise after the event. Nevertheless, for some years after they went into commission in 1927 these twelve ships gave me much hard work and worry.

They traded across the Atlantic to U.K. and Continental ports to discharge their petroleum cargoes shipped at Dutch West Indian ports, and as there were twelve of them there were sometimes two or more in a home or Continental port at the same time. Their unreliable engines invariably needed repairing when they arrived, so that my time was very fully occupied attending them. It was generally a case of travelling by night and working by day, and as the ships had a habit of arriving at week-ends, the recognised weekly breathing spell was denied me. As for summer holidays, the first for five years occurred in 1932. During those strenuous years I had many exciting and sometimes unpleasant experiences, but it will suffice to record three, which occurred within a space of three weeks towards the end of 1929.

At that time I had orders to proceed to the oil port of Stanlow, near Manchester, to investigate the difficulties one of these twelve ships was experiencing. After putting matters right I remained on board the ship during the passage through the Manchester Ship Canal towards Liverpool, to make quite sure that the engines were operating satisfactorily. Having, whilst at Stanlow, received instructions to proceed to Southampton at the earliest possible to attend to the troubles of another ship of the same class, I was anxious to get on my way.

When, therefore, the ship from Stanlow tied-up alongside the canal bank about 8 p.m. to await the opening of the lock gates at Eastham, situated at the western end of the canal, I thought to save a little time and make quite sure of catching my train connection at Birkenhead, by going over the side by a rope ladder and climbing the canal embankment. As soon as my foot left the bottom rung, the ladder was hauled up and the ship moved off into the darkness.

It had been raining heavily for days, and as soon as I began to climb the steep embankment I realised that it was not going to be easy to get to the top, even on all fours, as the embankment was made up of slippery clay. However, I persevered and was within a few feet of the top when my feet slipped and I slid lengthways to my starting point. The next attempt was more successful and I caught my train. It was then about 9 p.m. and I spent the whole of that night scraping the clay from my clothes with a penknife, arriving at Southampton about 2 p.m. the following day looking more like a potter than a Superintendent Engineer.

The difficulties experienced on the ship at Southampton occupied three days, during which time I worked continuously excepting for short breaks for meals and snatches of sleep on the settee in the Chief Engineer's cabin. The work completed, I found myself one of a few travellers on Southampton Station at noon on Christmas Day awaiting a train which would take me to Glasgow, having before leaving the ship received an urgent message to proceed to that port to attend another ship of the class which was also in difficulties.

The quickest way to Glasgow was via London and Newcastle, and I decided to break the journey at Newcastle and go home for a few hours. This decision was prompted partly by the desire for a really hot bath and a change of clothes, as I had then been hard at it away from home for nearly a fortnight, and all my clothes, and probably the part of me immediately under, were far from clean.

I arrived at Newcastle early on the morning of Boxing Day and proceeded to my home at Whitley Bay. After a good meal, a hot bath and a change of clothes, I left to catch the 11.14 a.m. train

I thought to save time and catch my train by going over the side by rope ladder and climbing the embankment.

from Newcastle. As the local trains were running very infrequently, it being a general holiday, I decided to make the journey to Newcastle in my car, arranging for my daughter to collect the car the next day from a garage adjoining the station.

Upon arriving at Newcastle station about 11 o'clock I learned that the 11.14 train was not running that day, it being Sunday service only, and that the next train would not leave until something after 2 p.m. Rather than wait about in the station which was cold and cheerless, I decided to return and spend the time at home.

Being Boxing Day I had the road between Newcastle and Whitley Bay more or less to myself. When approaching the Wallsend cross roads, two little chaps not more than six years old were running across an open piece of ground towards the road. As they were obviously not concerned with anything on wheels which might be coming along the road, I watched their progress and reduced speed to give them time to cross.

The boy who was leading the other by two or three paces ran on to the road without looking right or left, but when he got half way across he seemed to become conscious of a car approaching and stood still, as though to let it pass before continuing his journey to a sweet shop on the other side of the road. I would then be some thirty yards from the boys, travelling at about 20 miles an hour and ready to take whatever action was necessary to avoid colliding with them. By this time the second boy had stopped running and stood with, but on the far side of, his companion. Thinking that both boys were aware of my approach and were waiting for me to pass, I accelerated, but just as I got abreast of them the second boy, whom I could not see because he was behind his companion, ran right in front of the car.

The despair and anguish which swept over me when I felt the car wheels pass over the little body I will not attempt to describe. When I stopped some ten yards further on and jumped out of the car there he was lying in the middle of the road, his little friend having got such a fright that he ran away.

There was no one about who might help, so I picked up the boy and put him in the car, and although distracted, turned the car around and made for Newcastle Hospital with all possible speed.

His little body was so limp that I thought he must be dead. On arrival at the hospital he was taken straight into the accident ward and given every possible attention. After waiting a couple of hours, I left when assured that the boy still lived and that he was as comfortable as possible in the circumstances.

I then returned to the place where the accident occurred with the intention of finding out where the boy's parents lived. Seeing some men standing at the roadside I asked them if they had heard about a little boy being run over a couple of hours before. They said they had, and in answer to a further question told me that the name of the boy was Jimmy Mullen. I then asked where his parents lived and set off for the house indicated.

When I arrived at the home of the boy's parents the living room was full of people, mostly women, all talking loudly of the accident and every other accident they had heard or read about. A young woman sitting quietly by the side of the fire in great distress was obviously the Mother of the boy. I approached her, saying that she must bear up because her boy was in good hands. She replied between her sobs that it was not so, that she had been told he was dead and not nice to see. That anyone could be so unkind was incredible and made me angry. I refuted this lie as kindly as I could, and told her that I should know because I had taken her boy to the hospital and was the last to see him. Remembering that his name was Jimmy Mullen it fortunately occurred to me to say that if what she had been told was true, how did I, a complete stranger, know that his name was Jimmy Mullen ? That seemed to reassure her and she became less distressed.

I then decided to go to the police and tell what had happened. I asked the only man in the room, whom I presumed was the boy's father, if he would go with me, and the poor fellow said " Yes, if you will wait until I put a coat on." At that moment a policeman came to the door and asked if it was I who had taken the boy to the hospital. I replied " Yes." He then asked if I could give the number or a description of the car which knocked the boy down. I replied, " Yes, the number of the car is TY 2103." " But," he said, " that is the number of the car at the door, which I presume is yours." I said " You are right, that is the car which knocked him down." I then told him that I was about to go to the Police Station to make a statement, but he told me that as I had done everything possible for the boy's comfort it would be sufficient if I gave him my name and address and a few particulars of the accident.

After giving him the information required he mentioned that when he arrived on the scene of the accident shortly after it happened there were a few people standing around. In answer to his questions as to the type of vehicle involved, one said that it was a motor lorry, another that it was a saloon car and that another car had come along and taken the boy away, whilst another emphatically stated that she had seen the accident and that it was a motor cycle which had run over the boy !

It is now more years than I care to remember since I began driving a motor car and this has been my only accident, and when I recall the anxious moments and the nerve strain endured, those who have the misfortune to be involved in similar accidents always get my full sympathy, unless, of course, they are of the type who think that nobody should be on the road but themselves.

The boy's parents were in very straightened circumstances, as were many others at that time, the accident having occurred during the great trade slump. The father, a miner, had been gassed in World War I and was in receipt of a pension sufficient only to pay the rent of the small council house they lived in. He generally worked for a week or two in the pits and then had to lay-off for several weeks because his lungs troubled him. Their diet had for months before consisted almost solely of soups made from bones which were bought for a few coppers on Saturday nights at Newcastle meat market. Their only other child had died some two years before from meningitis, so that if ever a couple were deserving of help it was those two.

The outcome of this accident was that the father obtained a job as storekeeper at one of the engineering works on the Tyne, and Jimmy, the boy, completely recovered, later served his apprenticeship to engineering at the same works, ultimately proceeding to sea where he did well as an engineer officer.

Needless to say it was late on the night of that eventful Boxing

Day when I began my weary journey to Glasgow, arriving there just in time to catch the last bus proceeding in the direction in which I wanted to go. All I knew about my destination was that it was a little place called Kilpatrick, situated about half-way between Glasgow and Greenock.

It was a dreadful night. Glasgow at that time had a minimum of street lighting because of the need to economise. To add to the discomfort of those who had to be abroad so late it was bitterly cold, windy and the rain poured down. Never was I so thankful for the shelter of a stuffy bus, even though it meant sitting in wet clothes with my sorrowful thoughts. Was Jimmy still alive ? If alive, would he be crippled all his life ? Could I have done more ? If only the 11.14 train had run that day ; if only one of a hundred things had happened which would have prevented me being on that particular part of the road at that moment !

A man's voice enquiring " tickets please " made my thoughts jump some 180 miles in an instant. I told him I wanted to go to Kilpatrick oil installation. He had never heard of the oil installation, nor had anyone else in the bus, so all he could do, he said, was to put me down at Kilpatrick. The bus arrived there about midnight and I alighted, feeling that I would soon find the oil installation.

When I got off the bus the rain was still pouring down, and the wind howling so hard that no other sound could be heard. After the bus had got under way again and left me standing, there wasn't a light to be seen anywhere, not even a street light. More by instinct than by sight I realised that I was standing beside a row of houses abutting the pavement, and decided that the only course open to me was to wait until another who had to be afoot at such an hour on such a night chanced to come my way.

As it was raining heavily I naturally stood flat against one of the houses to miss as much of the rain and wind as possible. After a time I heard heavy footsteps approaching, and when the owner was within a couple of yards or so I stepped forward to enquire the way to the oil installation. The queston, however, was never given voice because the man evidently thought I had evil intentions. Without a word he ran off at top speed and left me gaping. After a further long wait, another man came along, but this time I stood out in the rain and called out to him before he got too near to me. He turned out to be a railwayman, and being made of sterner stuff than the other gentleman he stood his ground and directed me as best he could.

To get to the gates of the oil installation I had to walk along a narrow path between a canal and a railway track, which, owing to the heavy rain, strong wind and the darkness, proved a precarious undertaking. After moving inch by inch for some distance I concluded that if I proceeded I would finish up in the canal, and therefore retraced my steps. It was so dark, however, that I was unable to find my way back to the place where I had left the bus and eventually arrived at a signal cabin. After briefly explaining my predicament, the signalman, who was about to finish his spell of duty, said he would accompany me to the oil installation if I would wait a little while. The cabin gave shelter and warmth and I was tempted to ask permission to stay there until daylight, but we set off along the canal bank, which could be dimly seen by the light of a hurricane lamp which he carried. After about twenty minutes walk we arrived at the gates of the installation, and my guide, being anxious to get home and out of the rain, said " good night."

Turning to the gates I found to my dismay that they were locked, and taller than I could reach or see. Inside was a hut from which a light shone, so that all I could do was to try to attract the attention of the occupant by shouting as loudly as I could, but the howling wind and the noise of the rain evidently drowned my voice, since there was no response from the hut.

I then decided that there was nothing for it but to climb over the gates. All went well until I reached the top, when I found that the gates were about eight feet high and spiked. The violence of the wind and rain seemed to increase as I clung to those spikes, and just how long it took me to get over that gate without leaving some of my flesh behind I don't know, but eventually I managed to get to the other side with nothing worse than a few rents in my clothes and very sore hands and knees.

I banged open the door of the hut, in which a man was comfortably sleeping. Having roused him, he procured a lamp and we set out for the ship, arriving on board about two hours after I left the bus, literally soaked to the skin. After a hot bath and a few hours' sleep, in borrowed clothes I was ready to tackle the problems which were confronting the Chief Engineer of that particular ship. Two days later I was on my way to Genoa to attend to another " lame duck."

The saying " It is an ill wind which blows nobody any good " could, in the fullest sense, be applied to those ships. They must have cost the owners a fortune in repairs, and many headaches and sleepless nights to those of us who had to look after them. Nevertheless, they taught us a great deal about this new type of engine, knowledge which was doubtless put to good purpose in engines built subsequently, by the many engineers who so ably assisted in keeping them in serviceable condition. Moreover, they provided much needed work during the great trade slump of 1930-32, when the unusual sound of a rivetter's hammer in any of the great shipyards on the rivers Tyne and Clyde caused one to stop and listen.

Those twelve ships were generally drydocked on the Tyne by Hawthorn, Leslie & Co., Ltd., the famous shipbuilders and engineers. The one responsible for getting the work done in the shortest time and at the lowest cost was Mr., now Sir, Philip Johnson, a most likeable man and one who was to become a power in the industry, as exemplified by the honour conferred upon him by King George VI. Sir Philip was, and is still, after almost thirty years, not a pound heavier than was absolutely necessary, his leanness being accentuated by the fact that the bottom button of his jacket is always fastened. His stockily built, vigorous assistant, Mr. John Bulman, was characterised by his refusal to wear an overcoat, even on the coldest day. Anything, it seemed, which impeded in the least his desire to get on with the job could not be tolerated. Perhaps it was this particular trait in his character which enabled him to rise unaided from the lowest to the highest position in the factory in which he has been employed all his working life.

Owing to the depth of water and other conditions being

unsuitable at the place on the river where these ships lay when re-fitting, it was not possible to test the engine whilst the ship was moored to the jetty. Consequently we had to take her to sea in order to be certain that the work had been properly done. In all, those twelve ships must have left the Tyne in this unorthodox way over fifty times, and the fact that never once did a ship have to put back because of work improperly done, endorses the high standard of workmanship for which Hawthorn Leslie are renowned.

During some of the refits the huge complicated engines were stripped down to their foundations and re-built, involving the fitting together of hundreds of bits and pieces, some big, some small, some weighing tons and some ounces, but accuracy was of equal importance in every case. On such occasions, and they were frequent, it was my custom to stay on board until the ship reached a position off Dover. Sir Philip generally accompanied me as he was as anxious as I to be satisfied that the engines were in good seaworthy condition before the ship began the Atlantic crossing.

Those excursions could be very pleasant, but we didn't always disembark off Dover in daylight and fine weather. More often than not it was black dark, and a sizeable sea running. Strong winds and heavy rain would occasionally join in, just to make things a little more difficult.

The procedure when a ship was about to sail was to telegraph the shipping agents at Dover the expected time of arrival off that port, and request a launch to be sent out to take off passengers. In favourable weather the ship would stop within a mile or so of Dover harbour and a small motor boat would be sent to take us off. In adverse weather the ship would stand-off five to six miles and the larger and much more powerful pilot cutter would be sent out.

On more than one occasion my companion and I have stood on the deck of our ship sheltering from the cold wind and rain, trying to pierce the darkness for the first sight of a little light, which was all we could see of our launch leaving the harbour. Eventually the anxiously awaited light would appear, and if after a time it began behaving as if it were being used to send a message by morse code, we knew that it was the one we were waiting for, and that the launch was ploughing her way through the rough sea towards us.

On one such occasion it was so dark that it was not possible to see the pilot cutter, even when it reached the side of our rolling and pitching ship. The drenched men in the cutter could be heard shouting their loudest, but the howling wind and the noise of the cutter flopping in the sea made it impossible to hear what they wished us to know. Assuming that it was to hurry, before the weather got worse, I began the precarious descent down the rope ladder hanging over the side of the ship. After covering about ten feet I could make out the shape of the cutter, rising and falling alarmingly on the waves and every now and again crashing against the ship's side with a force that would have broken a less stout craft to matchwood.

At one moment the cutter would be at my feet and the next it would be six or more feet below me and out of sight. Had I descended further I would have run the risk of having my legs crushed by the ten ton cutter. I therefore clung to the swaying ladder with numbing hands, and eventually heard the skipper of the cutter shout " Hang on, then let go when I tell you." After the cutter had risen on the crest of the waves a number of times the injunction to " let go " was heard and, as I was expected to, I released my hold and fell blindly backwards into the strong arms waiting to catch me. Sir Philip was my companion on this occasion, and I was relieved when he boarded the cutter in like manner and with no more bruises than I had received.

CHAPTER XVI

WITS AND WISDOM

SOME of us have met at one time or another, the type of person who prefers to live by trading upon the gullibility of others rather than by earning an honest living. I met a member of this type only once. It happened on a Saturday afternoon whilst making a journey by train from Tilbury to London. When the train, which was of the non-corridor type, left Tilbury I was the sole occupant of a first class compartment. Having from the night before had a busy time on one of the ships for which I was technically responsible, I contented myself by reclining in the corner furthest away from the platform of the stations at which the train stopped, idly watching other passengers as they passed by the window.

At one station early on the journey a man entered my compartment and sat down in the corner opposite me. By selecting that particular corner of the three vacant he caused me to reluctantly draw in my tired outstretched legs. He was of a type which didn't interest me, so that when he passed the time of day I made a suitable reply, more out of politeness than a desire to converse with him. When, however, he disclosed a wish to know where I came from, where I was going and the nature of my business, I gave an evasive reply and picked up my newspaper. This move had the desired effect because he said no more whilst we were alone together.

When the train stopped at the next station three men in rather shabby sporty rig, and not of the kind one would expect to be travelling first class, entered the compartment. These men, one of herculean dimensions, sat down at the opposite end of the compartment and I was not surprised when their conversation centered on their experience at race meetings, not, I would add, for the purpose of seeing the horses race.

Presently the giant of the trio spread a newspaper over his bulky knees and brought out a pack of playing cards from his coat pocket. A discussion then arose as to the game they should play and finally it was agreed that they should play " threes." They amused me by the apparent serious thought given to the way in which they would while away the time, and although never a card player myself, I was curious to know how the game of " threes " was played.

The man sitting opposite to me indicated by a look that he also was amused. When we realised that it was a case of " find the lady " we exchanged glances and each picked up a newspaper to indicate to the card-sharpers that we were not interested in them or their game any longer. Nevertheless I was somewhat surprised at the audacity of these rogues to operate on a train which had so far stopped at every station. Whether it would continue to do so or not I did not know, but no doubt they did.

Soon after leaving the next station the man sitting opposite to me was asked to join in. His answer was a firm but polite refusal. The request was then put to me and I replied similarly. They again turned their attention to the man opposite, who gradually succumbed to their persuasions and with apparent reluctance joined in " for three rounds only," so he said. He won the first round, lost the second and won the third, which left him £6 better off. At this point I began to think he was one of them, but his determined refusal to play a fourth round reassured me.

During the argument that ensued it occurred to me that I had seen these three men before, particularly the big one. I remembered, also, that they had approached my compartment from the forward end of the train whereas other passengers had passed along the platform from the rear end, suggesting that prior to entering my compartment these crooks had been operating in compartments nearer the engine. This line of thought having started, I felt sure these three men had passed my compartment window at a previous station. Moreover, that it was at the station at which the man now sitting opposite me entered the compartment. What I could not remember was " did I see the trio before this man got in or after." If I could have been sure that I had seen the trio after the man opposite me entered, I would have known that he was the tout of the gang.

At this stage the man opposite leaned towards me and whispered " Let's go in and skin them," while his eyes indicated that he knew all the tricks in the game. He began to play without waiting to see if I would join in. Although his luck seemed to be in, I was quite content to sit and watch him " skin " them. After a few rounds the dealer flicked a card in such a way that it fell at my feet and the bulky one asked me to pick it up. This I did and threw it on to the newspaper spread across his knees.

Whilst picking up the fallen card I noticed that it was the Queen and that one corner had been turned over slightly. The three cards were then dealt, the dealer having taken care not to straighten out the corner of the winning card. I was again asked to "find the lady," and when the man opposite put his £5 on one of the other two cards I knew he was one of them, because I turned the face of the card towards him as I picked it up and he was bound to see the bent corner.

As the invitation to join in the game became more insistent I felt I had to retort, although it would have been wiser to have said nothing. What I said was " Do you think I am completely dumb, I know where the lady is as you all do, because you have marked her." This was a bad move, since like a shot, the dealer put his finger on the marked card saying " You're on this one," turned it face up and counted out ten £1 notes, all in a much shorter time than it takes to tell. He then tried to thrust the money into my hand, saying " This is yours, take it," to which I replied pushing the money away from me, " It isn't mine and I doubt if it is rightfully yours."

This remark seemed to infuriate the rogue, or at any rate gave him the excuse for appearing to be so, because he jumped to his feet and stood towering over me. Knowing by this time that they were all in league with one another and that I had about £40 in my pocket, I didn't relish the situation, especially as I knew that the great mass of humanity forcing me into the corner could quite easily stop me from getting at the communication cord. Moreover, they were now all on their feet and adopting a threatening attitude. I frankly admit to not having been so frightened since the day I went to have my first tooth pulled out.

He tried to thrust the money into my hand.

The train, according to schedule I suppose, began to pass station after station and it seemed as though I would either have to play or be beaten-up. I therefore agreed to play, and thought to make each game spin out as long as possible. One difficulty I foresaw was to extract a few notes from my wallet without disclosing how much money I had with me. I didn't have to find a way of doing this, however, for they seemed to have lost all desire to play and the situation took an unpleasant turn.

Just as they were about to put their hands on me the train, by a strange and fortunate coincidence, began to lose speed rapidly and stopped. I was so hemmed in by the mass of low humanity that I couldn't see where we were. After about a minute or so, during which time not a word was spoken, the train began moving again and almost before I had time to realise what was happening I was alone in the compartment.

I learnt later that the train had unexpectedly stopped at a station, not because it was a station but because the signal was against it. For reasons which I cannot explain, the card-sharpers kept quite quiet until the train began to move, when they jumped out. A possible explanation is that by delaying their departure in this way I would not be able to follow them. Why they didn't stay and carry out their evil intention of robbing me before reaching the next station is beyond me to explain, as they held all the cards in more ways than one. The next station was Fenchurch Street, the terminus, and the explanation may be that it would be too difficult to escape before the alarm could be raised.

When I realised what had happened I rushed to the carriage door and saw the quartette hurrying towards the platform exit. Apart from them and a solitary porter at the other end, the platform was deserted. The porter was standing shouting something in a very tired voice, and as my carriage came abreast of him, I was amused to hear him warning passengers that there were card-sharpers on the train. As I passed him I couldn't refrain from shouting " There were," and pointing in the direction of the exit.

CHAPTER XVII

TAKING A CHANCE

THE beginning of the year 1938 found me still a Superintendent Engineer, having served the same employers for nineteen years. I was in receipt of a good salary with conditions of employment the best to be found anywhere. The work was hard but it was still interesting, even though I had been doing it for fourteen years.

Many would, no doubt, have been content to continue until reaching retiring age, but I became restive. This was solely due to there being no prospects of further promotion because, I was told, there was an understanding between the British and larger foreign interests of the Company, that the next higher position should be held by a representative of the foreign country concerned.

It was difficult to know what to do. I was happy in my job which gave good returns and security, while on the other hand the desire within me to progress further was still an active driving force. Moreover, I felt that if I did not make a move before reaching the age of fifty — I was then forty-eight — I might think myself too old to take the risk. The thought of doing until reaching retiring age, what I had been doing for so long, did not appeal to me a bit, and I began looking around for an opening which would afford scope for advancement.

My immediate superior was a capable engineer about seven years my senior, very tall and lean but otherwise not outwardly attractive. Never did I see such long legs take such short strides so quickly. While he had some good qualities, patience was not one of them, which no doubt accounted for his peculiar walk and jerkiness in speech and actions. Nevertheless, whilst he could not claim to be universally popular with his business associates, he and I got on very well together. Many were the occasions when we did not see eye to eye on technical problems, but on personal matters there were no differences.

Having made the decision to seek other employment I at once advised my Chief of my intention. We had finished talking business when I said there was a personal matter about which I wished to speak to him. Almost before I had finished saying " I wish to resign," he became angry and told me not to be silly. " No one " he said, " with any sense ever leaves this Company." How many times he repeated these uncomplimentary remarks I don't know, and as it was apparent that he was not going to listen to me I left his room, intending to make a further approach next morning. The next day was the last of a month, and as I wished to terminate my employment at the end of the following month it was necessary to resign officially without delay.

This approach, however, never materialised, because he had in the meantime left for the Continent. I therefore wrote out my resignation and sent it by hand to the Secretary of the Company. Within an hour the Managing Director sent for me, and in kindly broad Scots asked me to give him more details of the reason for taking such an unusual step. He listened so patiently to what I had to say that I was encouraged to tell him not only what he wanted to know, but of my hopes for the future. Like all great industrial leaders he was economical in the use of words, so it did not surprise me when he merely said " Sound reasoning, and I won't ask you to reconsider your decision on the promise of a substantial increase in salary, so good-bye and good luck."

As I was leaving the room a dark complexioned, immaculately dressed man of about my own age approached me. He must have been standing in a secluded part of the room during the interview as I had not previously noticed him. He handed me a visiting card and said " The best of luck in your new venture. Let me know from time to time how you are getting on." Noting the friendly expression on his shrewd face I resolved to do so. The name on the card was familiar to me, but it wasn't until a few days later that I learned that he was the new Managing Director.

When my Chief returned I sought an early interview, so that I could tell him of the action I had taken and my reasons for doing so. He, however, refused to see me and would take no part in the pleasing little ceremony planned by my colleagues, when they presented me with a beautiful gold cigarette case.

Some time before sending in my resignation, I had been told that Johnny Horton was looking for a partner. This grand little man was Mr. J. C. V. Horton, Managing Director of a firm of Consulting Engineers and Marine Surveyors. After an exchange of letters we met, and he offered me a third share in a business that was all but dead. Practically all reserves of capital had been used up and the Company was a mere skeleton of its former self.

Two things attracted me, however, one was that the business was the oldest of its kind in the country, having been established in 1891, and the other that it certainly offered unlimited scope for new ideas and determined effort.

The only other partner in the business was the widow of a late Director, whose interest did not extend beyond visiting the office once each year to attend the annual Board meeting. Mr. Horton, who was a trained naval architect had joined the firm as an office boy some forty-five years earlier, and had served under two principals of outstanding capabilities whose names the firm now bore. The last of these, however, had died some years before I became interested in the results of their labours.

When I took up my new duties in March 1938, the Company had the technical supervision of three ships, which brought in £300 annually. This sum was hardly enough to pay office rent and support two working directors, one sleeping director, a shorthand typist and an office boy. The need to secure new business was, therefore, extremely urgent, particularly as it had been broadly hinted that the only three ships on the books would pass into the care of others at the end of the year.

Notices that I had joined the Company appeared in all technical journals, and letters were sent to all likely firms to make use of our services. Also, I lost no time calling upon our only client, but could not get definite assurance that they would not hand over the technical supervision of their three ships to someone else. Time passed, and nobody offered us work. We did not in fact receive a single enquiry, and it became apparent that if we were to get work I would have to go out and fetch it.

Canvassing was not in my line, and after a month with nothing

to show for my efforts I could not claim to be very adept,
Nevertheless, I learnt a good deal in that first month. One thing
was that the people who were in a position to give us work were
mostly non-technical, so that it was no use talking to them in the
language I knew best. I had to acquire their language, which was
£ s. d., and try to prove that I could save lots for them if they
would let me supervise the construction of their contemplated
ships, or technically manage any they might have in service.

Before approaching prospective clients I took good care to get
to know as much as I could from published records about their
ships and the trade in which they were interested. Another thing
I learned was to keep my pride in my pocket, otherwise it would
have been severely trampled on. More than once I had my
visiting card returned with the words " I don't want to see you "
or some such curt message scribbled across it.

If I had good reasons for knowing that the writers of such
messages contemplated placing orders for new ships, I would not
take the rebuke as final and would continue to call and present my
card until I obtained an interview. Such persistence bore fruit on
more than one occasion. The one that comes readily to mind
concerns a man who had sent shipbuilders enquiries for the
construction of two new ships. After many fruitless calls, this
man condescended to see me, not, it soon became apparent, to
hear what I knew about ships, but to tell me what he knew, or
thought he knew. In business circles he was recognised as a
shrewd man and his achievements in shipowning proved this
opinion of him to be correct.

After listening to a good deal of nonsense about how ships and
engines should be constructed, I decided that one of two courses
was open to me. Either I should agree and keep on a friendly
footing with him, or disagree and be thrown out. I reasoned that
if I did adopt the first course there was no certainty that I would
get what I wanted, as he might very well feel he had been
reassured that he was qualified to look after the building of the
ships himself. I therefore adopted the second course and began
by asking, most respectfully, highly technical questions about
ships, which I knew he could not answer. Some of the questions

he would have ignored if I had let him, while he made valiant
attempts to answer others. Being ostensibly out to help him, I
took pains to show where he was wrong, and after an hour or so
he suddenly remembered an important appointment and asked to
be excused.

I went away feeling that nothing would come of this meeting,
but wait, he did shake hands with me on parting ! A week passed,
and then I received a telephone message asking me to call and see
him immediately. Needless to say I lost no time in answering the
call, and when shown into the great presence the greeting was not
" good afternoon " or " how are you," but " What would be your
fee for looking after the building of my two ships ? " Without
hesitation I said " Quarter of one per cent. of the contract price."
His immediate reply was " Too much, I'll give you one eighth of
one per cent.," with a gesture which clearly said take it or leave it.
Being badly in need of work and remembering the old axiom that
half a loaf is better than no bread, I accepted.

After the agreement had been signed, I made a careful study of
the shipbuilders' specification and was able to propose a number
of amendments. This pleased my client, particularly as the
shipbuilders, who turned out to be very accommodating, had
agreed to provide the additions and modify certain other items
without extra cost to the purchaser. A few months later my new
client asked me to survey a ship he was thinking of buying, and
as I was able to help him very materially in making a good
purchase, he began to think that it was well to have a technical
man around when building or buying ships.

By the time the first of the two new ships was ready for launching, my client had become quite amenable, and when he saw the
first ship completed and on sea trials I was afraid he would lose
control to the extent of embracing me. On the way from the ship
he did in fact put an arm on my shoulder and say, " Look here
John, I treated you badly when we first met and I am going to
make amends by paying you the fee you asked." I replied
" Thanks, that is a gesture I appreciate, but my fee in the case of
these two ships is one-eighth of one per cent. The next ships,
however, if there are are any, will be one-quarter of one per

cent." That my client was sincere was proved on completion of the second ship when he gave me a very lovely present.

In the meantime more work had come our way, and at the end of two years we had the supervision of three large ships under construction, the technical management of eleven ships in service, and the modernising of a big water distilling plant in Aden. We had also been appointed consultants by a large firm manufacturing aluminium castings, and one of the world's largest shipping companies, besides acting as technical experts in several disputes which went to arbitration. The income from these sources was running at the rate of nearly £10,000 per annum.

By this time the Second World War had started and arrangements had been made for the position in my old Company to which I had aspired, to be filled by a Britisher. I was, in consequence, offered the position of Chief Marine Superintendent, an offer which was exceedingly attractive, but one which required some careful thought in view of the success which had rewarded my endeavours during the previous two years. In the end I felt that I could make a more useful contribution to the war effort with my old Company, and I returned to them in May 1940 after having got a capable engineer to assist my little friend, Johnny Horton, during the trying years which lay ahead.

CHAPTER XVIII

SO NEAR AND YET SO FAR

WHAT with wars and the inadequacy of our roads to ensure safe transit of careful as well as careless users, many of us have seen fellow humans meet an untimely end. The impression produced by such events depends in a large measure upon where the event takes place. If we ourselves are in danger, as on the battlefield, a sinking ship or in an air-raid, what we see and hear does not make such a deep impression as when the event takes place in peaceful surroundings.

I have witnessed many incidents wherein lives have been lost. In April 1912, I happened to be serving on a ship which reached the scene of the *Titanic* disaster within twenty-four hours of that fine ship sinking, with the loss of over one thousand five hundred lives. When we reached the scene, bodies supported by life-belts were floating all around, but I think the incident which produced the deepest impression was seeing a man drown in peaceful surroundings and being powerless to render assistance.

It happened when I and some thirty others were on board a slow old paddle tugboat early on a winter's evening in 1944. We had been running speed trials with a new ship off the Isle of Arran, and the trials having been successfully completed, the tug was taking us ashore, the ship having proceeded on its way.

When nearing the mouth of the Clyde, a very smart American cruiser passed us, making for the river. She was a pretty sight in the setting sun, and, amongst other things, my casual attention was attracted by three or four sailors wearing lifebelts at work over the stern. The cruiser was too far away for us to be sure what they were doing, but they appeared to be making something fast, or they might have been bringing depth charges inboard for safety while the ship was in port.

Although the evening was fine there was a moderate wind blowing, and the sea was what might be called choppy by those in a boat, but rough by those who had to swim in it. Presently something fell from the stern of the cruiser and the cry " man overboard " went up from the tug. All eyes turned as fingers were pointed in the direction of a small black object in the water astern of the cruiser, which was then about a quarter of a mile away and travelling at about six knots. The unfortunate man's companions could be seen running towards the bridge, giving the alarm by waving their arms, and doubtless shouting, but the cruiser covered probably half a mile before it could be stopped and a motor boat lowered to the water.

We little thought then that the incident would have a tragic end, because the man was wearing a lifebelt, and a motor boat, the speed and manoeuvrability of which we watchers admired, would we felt sure, soon be racing in his direction. Whilst we could see the man clearly every now and again from the tug, the men in the motor boat evidently could not, because they were altering course every few seconds and not getting any nearer to the unfortunate sailor. Once or twice the boat did proceed in the right direction and the tension felt by all on the tug, and no doubt all on the cruiser also, was relieved, but they altered course almost immediately, proving that they had not sighted their objective.

Realising this, the skipper of the tug headed in the man's direction, and after what seemed a long time to us, but wasn't really, got within a few hundred yards of him. The poor chap was in a panic judging by his cries and the frantic efforts he was making to reach the tug, but before we could get near enough to throw him a line he became exhausted and his head fell forward.

Such a sad end would doubtless have been avoided if the unfortunate man had had faith in his lifebelt, which would have supported him until help came to his aid. All he had to do was to remain still and float. Instead, he struggled hard to save himself struggles which it was apparent to everyone but himself were quite useless. In doing so he expended so much energy that after probably not more than twenty minutes he hadn't the strength to hold up his head. I wonder what I would have done in similar circumstances ?

CHAPTER XIX

PREPARING A WARM RECEPTION

ABOUT the middle of 1940 when we faced alone the might of Germany and an attempted invasion of these islands seemed imminent, our inimitable Prime Minister, Winston Churchill, called a meeting of Service Chiefs to decide upon the steps to be taken to frustrate such an undertaking. Our Intelligence Service it was stated, had advised that the Germans intended transporting their invading army in merchant ships, and that each of these ships would, in addition, have on board a very large number of collapsible canvas boats of ingenious construction, each capable of carrying one or two men with necessary fighting equipment. These ships, presumably escorted by warships, were to proceed to, and anchor off several of our beaches at the same time, when the enemy hoped the canvas boats on the ships that got through would be launched in smooth water and a landing effected.

Being a matter chiefly for the Royal Navy, the First Sea Lord, the late Sir Dudley Pound, was stated to be of the opinion that in view of our depleted naval strength the only way to stop them would be to set the sea around likely landing beaches on fire with petroleum. When asked how, he, it is said, frankly admitted that he did not know, but that it was the only certain way to prevent a landing. Sir Andrew Agnew, one of the great leaders of the Petroleum Industry, was then consulted and he selected six people, including myself, to carry out experiments with a view to finding out how portions of the sea could be set on fire without damage to our shores.

The team included a University Professor, a Naval Captain, a Petroleum Chemist, an Army Colonel and a Nautical Adviser. After a few meetings in London to decide upon a plan and make preliminary arrangements, the team journeyed North to Glasgow, where further discussions took place with the Admiral of that Port, the matters discussed being concerned with obtaining equipment and selecting a suitable site for the experiments. The

Admiral thought Sir Dudley's idea great and he proved most helpful. Moreover, our work had been given top priority, so we had no difficulty in getting all we wanted, which included a small tanker, a fairly large tug, a fast motor launch, high pressure pumps and large quantities of various grades of petroleum.

Arriving at the site recommended by the Admiral of the Port, no time was lost in making small scale tests in a large concrete water tank specially built for the purpose. These first tests proved how very difficult it would be to make even highly inflamable petrol burn unless poured on the water in quantities so large as to make the scheme impracticable.

Petrol would readily ignite providing the film on the water was of measurable thickness, but it quickly burnt away. Heavy fuel oil, on the other hand, would burn much more slowly but it was difficult to ignite. Our early endeavours were, therefore, concerned with finding the best compromise, i.e. the proportions of various grades of petroleum and other substances which could be ignited with certainty and which would burn reasonably slowly. At the same time special igniting apparatus had to be devised and made, as it was found that naked lights were too dangerous and an ordinary electric spark inadequate.

It soon became apparent that our main difficulty was the tendency of oil to spread readily to a very thin film, in which condition it was difficult to ignite, and when it did ignite the flame was soon extinguished because of the cooling effect of the water on which it floated. We had been told that if attempted, invasion would take place during the periods of short daylight, which meant winter time when the temperature of the sea near our coast line would not be higher than 40°F.

Our chief problem was, therefore, to prevent the oil being cooled below its ignition point and the fire extinguished before all the oil had been burnt. To do this the oil had to be of appreciable depth, and to obtain the desired depth the oil would have to be prevented from spreading. As it would be impossible to burn oil on open waters such as surround our beaches, the only alternative was to endeavour to produce a wall of fire that would extend between the headlands at each side of bays likely to be selected by the enemy.

Innumerable ideas to enclose the oil were tried out, but with only partial success. The best of all comprised two long sheets of fire-proof material made buoyant by means of floats and weighted so that they would float vertically and form a narrow channel, the upper edges projecting a few inches above the water. This idea failed because the heat produced by the oil burning in the channel was so intense that the portion of the material above the water became charred and fragile after a short time, and allowed the oil to spread. The problem was accentuated by the possibility of the sea being in a disturbed or even a rough state during the attempted landing. With a wind blowing from seaward the burning oil might easily spread toward the beaches and do extensive damage.

After this series of tests we felt that if there was a solution to the problem it lay in a different direction from the one we had been pursuing so diligently. There was no shortage of ideas, but as each was discussed it was abandoned for some reason or other until in the end it seemed as though we would have to admit failure.

Then one day as I sat tired and dirty on the deck of the tug boat turning things over in my mind, my eye fell upon a piece of discarded cocoanut matting about six foot by three foot floating on the water in front of and within a few feet of me. Without any particular intention I picked up a large syringe, filled it from a bucket within reach containing the mixture of petroleum which had been found to be the most burnable on water, and idly sprayed the cocoanut matting. I then touched the matting with the igniter, and noted with interest how quickly the oil ignited and how rapidly the fire spread over the whole surface of the matting.

The second interesting thing noted was that the fire did not extend beyond the confines of the matting even though it was surrounded by a thin film of oil floating on the water. Other features which attracted my attention were the unusually long time the fire burnt fiercely for the small amount of oil squirted on to the matting, while after the fire had burnt out the upper surface of the matting was not even scorched by the intense heat. This seemed to be a matter worth investigating, and after my colleagues had assembled, I repeated the operation and they were no less impressed than I had been, particularly when we later found that with intermittent spraying of the matting the fierce fire could be maintained indefinitely with a remarkably small expenditure of oil.

The idea of using cocoanut matting to contain the oil was developed step by step, until it was found possible to quickly unroll on the surface of the water a 100 foot long coil of matting, to one side of which was attached a flattened hose made of special fabric. When laid the hose was underneath the matting, and as oil was forced into one end it assumed a circular form and the oil escaped through a line of small equally spaced holes. The oil, being lighter than water, rose to the surface and saturated the matting.

Before this stage was reached many difficulties had to be overcome. For instance, the matting had to be woven as thin as possible to reduce bulk without sacrificing buoyancy, the material for the oil feeding hose had to be almost paper thickness yet strong enough to withstand appreciable internal pressure, while the feeding holes in the hose had to be large enough to keep the fire going with the minimum consumption of oil.

The usefulness of this method of producing a controllable wall of fire on water was, however, limited to about a hundred feet owing to the insurmountable difficulty of ensuring the oil travelling along the hose for a greater distance at uniform pressure.

Although a big step forward had been made, we were a long way from fulfilling official requirements. These were to produce a wall of fire of a length which would extend across all beaches likely to be used for landing, the distances involved being up to two miles. Moreover, the heat produced had to be sufficiently great to deter invaders from diving underneath the fire and swimming ashore, and, finally, the fire had to burn for twelve hours at least, as this was the length of time necessary for our naval forces to reach the scene and deal with the enemy in the more orthodox manner.

After carefully reviewing the results so far obtained, it was decided to develop the use of cocoanut matting further, as the peculiar properties of this material seemed to offer the best chances of success.

Various ideas were put forward by different members of the team, and the scheme finally envisaged was to run out matting in the form of a trough eighteen inches deep which could be filled with oil as it was run out from the ship. To give the matting this form, it was to be reinforced by interweaving lengths of round iron wire transversely through the matting every twelve inches of its length, and press it into shape by machinery situated in the stern of the ship.

Small scale tests were first carried out with a cocoanut matting box about eight foot long and eighteen inches wide and deep. The box floated on the surface of the water even though its weight had been increased by the iron wire stiffeners. As oil was poured into the box it was found that although the matting was as porous as a wicker basket when out of the water, the oil did not leak out nor did water leak in. This peculiar property of cocoanut matting suited our purpose admirably. Moreover, when filled, the weight of the oil plus the weight of the box was equal to the depth of water displaced, consequently the oil in the box was at the same level as the water outside.

When ignited the oil burnt fiercely but as the quantity of oil was reduced the box rose out of the water and the matting above the water level burnt away, allowing the oil to overflow. How to keep the box submerged was the immediate problem. After much thought and many trials it was found that if two inch diameter holes spaced one foot apart were cut in the bottom of the box, water entered and replaced the oil at the same rate as the oil burnt away. Thus the problem of keeping the trough submerged as the oil burnt away was solved.

At this stage sufficient information had been obtained to justify the claim, that if desired a channel of oil could be quickly laid in water, for a distance limited only by the amount of coconut matting and oil which could be accommodated in shallow draught ships. As only small ships could be used at the points at which they were intended to operate, the quantities of these commodities must be reduced to an absolute minimum. Means had to be found, therefore, which would reduce the thickness of the matting and the burning rate of the oil.

A trough of oil eighteen inches deep burnt away in just over two hours, which was much too short a time. Increasing the depth of the oil channel would lengthen the burning time, but there were objections to obtaining the desired results in this way. It meant a greater bulk of matting and more oil.

Attempts to reduce the burning rate by altering the proportions of the different grades of petroleum composing the mixture failed, and numerous other ideas were tried out. Finally it was found that by laying muslin on the surface of the oil the burning rate was reduced very considerably. Moreover, that the rate could be increased or decreased at will by varying the mesh of this commonly used material, the smaller the mesh the lower the burning rate. As the burning rate was reduced the height of the flames and the amount of heat radiated became less, but ultimately a fire could be produced which burnt fiercely enough to stop any invader and for a time that would enable our naval forces to reach the scene.

When burning uncontrolled, the flames reached a height of over fifty feet, and the heat was so intense that the fire could not be approached, even momentarily, to within a distance of fifty yards unless we were clothed in asbestos suits and helmets.

So far as " playing with fire " was concerned our work had been accomplished. We had many exciting and some rather terrifying experiences, but apart from singed eyebrows and scorched skin there were no casualties. On looking back this is surprising, because at times, when about to make an important discovery, members of the team became so excited that proper precautions were not always taken. The greatest risks occurred when large scale tests were made to ascertain the alterations necessary to reduce the burning rate of the oil. On such occasions, a hundred foot long raging fire would be produced, and in order to see clearly what was happening between the surface of the oil and the flame it was necessary to approach as near as possible to the fire. The practice was to don fire-resisting clothes and board the fast motor boat. When all other precautions had been taken we would dash off straight for the fire, and alter course by forcing the rudder hard over only when the intense heat and rarified air made it physically impossible to remain a moment longer.

The next step was to design equipment to be fitted into existing ships. The work of producing plans went on night and day, and within five months of being assigned to the task, the first ship was equipped and ready for trial. The principle proved to be sound, and after a few minor alterations had been made to the trough-laying and igniting parts of the equipment, it was rather uncanny, but a very satisfying sight to watch this ship moving along at about four knots and laying behind it a really terrifying wall of fire. Many factors not mentioned here had to be taken into account, one of the most important being the tendency for the fire to creep up to the ship. This risk was eliminated by finding means of controlling the rate at which the fire spread along the channel, and in this connection an essential condition was that the ship's speed should be exact and consistent.

CHAPTER XX

OIL TANKERS IN WAR-TIME

FROM 1940 to the end of the Second World War in 1945 I held the position of Chief Marine Superintendent with The Anglo-Saxon Petroleum Company, then, as now, one of the largest shipping companies in the world. As such I was technically responsible for the operation and repair of the ships, their machinery and equipment, as well as the construction of new ships.

Of the 208 ships owned by the Company and its subsidiaries at the beginning of the war, 87 were sunk and 50 seriously damaged, the respective cargo carrying capacities being 689,661 and 493,535 tons. Some 1,750 officers, seamen and naval gunners lost their lives in those ships, while many more were permanently, and sometimes horribly maimed.

The heavy casualties were due to commanders of enemy submarines and aircraft being instructed to single out and destroy the oil carrying ships sailing in convoys, because the German High Command knew that their cargoes were the life-blood of our nation. Without imported petroleum and its many by-products it would have been impossible for Britain and her allies to have carried the war to a successful conclusion.

Oil tankers are more strongly built than other ships, with the exception of warships, and will take considerable punishment before sinking. Because of this many of our seriously damaged ships limped or were towed into ports where they were repaired and returned to service. Sometimes only half the ship would reach port, whilst the middle portion of others was so torn and twisted by as many as three torpedoes that the old ends had to be joined to an entirely new middle part. Some ships were severely mauled and repaired as many as three times and were still in active service when the end of the war came. One was torpedoed and whilst making for the repair port was again torpedoed. In spite of having two holes in her sides, either of which was big enough to allow a double decker bus to pass through, she arrived safely.

My chief worry was the inflammable nature of the cargoes carried and the fear that the petroleum would be set on fire when a ship was torpedoed, bombed or mined. Tankers caught fire all too frequently, and if the cargo comprised petrol or the like the poor fellows on board stood very little chance of survival, as the lifeboats, their only means of escape, were quickly made useless by the fierce flames. If they did manage to lower the lifeboats their end was only delayed, as the burning oil, amounting to 1,000 tons or more, spread rapidly for hundreds of feet all around the ship.

When their cargoes comprised the heavier grades of petroleum the risk of fire was less, but it frequently happened that the lifeboat launching gear became covered with thick oil projected upwards by the force of the explosion, making it impossible to hold the slippery ropes, and the lifeboats capsized. The only chance then was to jump overboard to avoid going down with the ship. On such occasions some of the men would manage to scramble on to rafts or drifting lifeboats, but as they were invariably covered in thick oil, not only were they partially blinded, but they were doomed to slow asphyxiation owing to the pores of the skin becoming clogged.

Most of the men in our ships were personally known to me, and having had a gruelling experience at sea in the 1914-18 War, I lived through the terrible ordeals these poor fellows had to endure each time news was received of a ship having been attacked. At one period the dreaded news came twice, and sometimes thrice, in the same week and the solemn act of removing well-known ships' names from the active list had to be undertaken. Then would follow anxious days, waiting to know how the men had fared and which of them had made the supreme sacrifice.

The terrible ordeals endured by the men never left my mind for long, even though no-one in London at that time knew if they would be a victim of the next bomb to fall. Much was done to give the men at sea a better chance of getting away with their lives. For example, one day it occurred to me that it might be possible to produce soap which would be soluble in sea water. If so, the men in ships carrying viscous oil would be able to wash the oil from their bodies should they have to choose between jumping overboard or going down with the ship.

There was already on the market a liquid called " Teepol " which had this property, but in such form it would be of very little use to the men at sea. The Technical Products Department of the Shell Group was approached, and after a time " Teepol " in paste form became available. A serious disadvantage, however, was that it caused intense irritation of the user's eyelids. After many unsuccessful tests, my good friend Dr. Weidner suggested that castor oil would afford the necessary protection to the eyes. Having a blind eye, I acted as guinea-pig, and soon afterwards all ships' lifeboats and liferafts were provided with complete cleansing outfits, which if properly used would enable the men to wipe the fuel oil from their eyes, apply castor oil and then wash themselves in sea water.

Many other measures too numerous to describe here were introduced with the object of saving life or alleviating suffering, but there seemed little we could do for the men on petrol carrying ships when they caught fire. With very few exceptions, all lifeboats on oil tankers were made of wood. Steel boats had not been adopted prior to the war because they were susceptible to corrosion in sea air. When war came it was a matter for regret that lifeboats had not been made of steel, which at that time was thought to be the most suitable material under war conditions.

As matters became worse the Ministry of War Transport suggested that a concerted endeavour might be made to design a fireproof non-sinkable lifeboat for the petrol carrying ships. This at first seemed impossible, but the proposal was given serious consideration. To relate how this seemingly impossible task was ultimately accomplished, I cannot do better than reproduce an extract from the book " Tanker Fleet " written by the celebrated author W. E. Stanton-Hope. This reads as follows :—

"Obviously, human intervention was impossible in such an exceptional and tragic case. In other incidents, lives were lost that might have been saved had there been the means for protecting men until they were well clear of the ship. One of the gravest dangers was of oil seeping out upon the sea from damaged tanks and becoming ignited. There were occasions when fierce flames rising from surface petrol round a torpedoed tanker burned the lifeboats and falls, and proved fatal to those men who sought to escape by jumping overboard.

This situation was a challenge to all interested in saving life at sea, and Mr. H. C. T. Bryant, of the Tanker Tonnage Committee of the Petroleum Board, suggested that tankers should be provided with unsinkable fire-proof lifeboats. A technical panel under the Chairmanship of Mr. John Lamb, Chief Marine Superintendent of The Anglo-Saxon Petroleum Company, was appointed to investigate the matter. The panel produced plans for an all-steel, fire-proof lifeboat, which were ultimately approved by the Ministry of War Transport. Since it became obvious that tankers could not be supplied with these steel lifeboats for a considerable time, Mr. Lamb decided to see what could be done with existing wooden lifeboats, and it was due to his skill and perseverance that such lifeboats were converted successfully. Consider the problems which confronted him. The lifeboats had to be given greater buoyancy. They must be so modified as to come to no harm by being lowered into a sea of flame, and survive the tremendous heat of an oil fire for a fairly lengthy period. Necessarily, the crew must enter the boat before it was lowered, and then be given protection from the heat until clear of the danger zone. To safeguard them, it seemed they must be in an enclosed space, which meant that a new method of lowering the boat must be devised, and also a special device for releasing the falls.

As wooden oars could not be used over an area of blazing oil, consideration had to be given to alternative means of propulsion which could be used by the crew while remaining under cover. There was also the question of getting material and equipment in quantity during the war, and of the speediest way of producing and distributing fire-proof boats on a large scale for the tanker fleets.

With regard to this last-named problem, an early decision was taken. Instead of building new lifeboats, it was decided to convert those already in service, thereby saving valuable time and labour. To solve the many other problems of safeguarding lives from oil fires at sea, Mr. John Lamb and his colleagues converted a standard twenty-four foot clinkerbuilt wooden lifeboat into a fire-resisting craft for experimental purposes. Features of the converted boat were galvanised metal plates above the water line, metal coamings fixed to the gunwales to provide extra freeboard, and raised turtle decks at bow and stern. The great part of each side of the boat was 'blistered'— that is, given a bulge which, in this case, consisted of slab cork pegged together, wrapped in asbestos material and protected by galvanised sheet steel.

The hooks for lowering the boat on the falls were placed fore and aft on the steel turtle decks, together with the Mills patent releasing gear. This gear was chosen because neither end could be released until the boat was afloat fairly, thereby eliminating risk of the craft being capsized or swamped during the launching. Access to the fall hooks was through small watertight hatches in the turtle deck, and releasing the boat from the falls took only a moment.

To enclose the crew a concertina-like canopy was rigged in three sections, each operated independently. This was made of a special mixture of cotton and asbestos, the best fire-resisting material obtainable for the purpose. The canopy could be closed to cover the entire well of the lifeboat, the fore and aft portions moved by hand along metal tracks and the centre part operated by a miniature winch. In this way, the boat could be covered within the space of five seconds.

Another important device was a system of spray-pipes from which numerous jets of water played over the canopy and steel decks. Thus the whole exposed surface of the boat was kept continually wet to prevent it taking fire, and the sprays also served the purpose of keeping down the temperature inside the boat. The water was drawn through seacocks and fed to the outlet holes by two semi-rotary hand-pumps.

The means adopted to propel the boat was the device known as Fleming's patent hand-propelling gear, by which members of the crew moved levers to and fro thereby revolving the small propeller. Once clear of the burning oil area, the canopy could be shut concertina-like in its three sections, leaving the well of the boat open and enabling oars to be used or a sail hoisted. Other gadgets were fitted and improvements were made that gave the fire-proof lifeboat sailing qualities superior to the ordinary kind. Many tests had to be made before the boat was practical, and Mr. John Lamb, who supervised these, decided on a final experiment before permitting reproduction of the type for use by tankers.

' Experiment ' was a modest choice of description. His idea was nothing less than to subject his converted boat to an ordeal by fire under conditions closely resembling those which had already cost the lives of many tankermen at sea. Such was his faith in the work accomplished that he insisted on being in the lifeboat himself during the last exhaustive test, and his technical assistants, Mr. J. G. Robinson and Mr. A. Logan, sharing his confidence, volunteered to accompany him.

This spectacular experiment took place at a northern port, where the lifeboat was floated in a large concrete tank nearly full of water. A large quantity of motor spirit, diesel oil and fuel oil was then poured in and ignited, and Mr. Lamb and his colleagues entered the boat, closed the asbestos canopy and set the water-sprays going. A few privileged onlookers were present and members of the National Fire Service stood by with hoses. A light breeze fanned the flames ; the whole surface of the tank became a roaring inferno, and volumes of black smoke soon screened the boat from view.

It was expected that at any moment shrill blasts would be heard from the whistle Mr. Lamb had taken with him for use in emergency. No sound was heard indicating distress, and when the fire died out, the adventurers emerged from the boat little the worse for their experience and exulting over the result. Tests for temperature showed that the heat of the oil fire had reached 2,400 degrees Fahrenheit, while thermometers inside the lifeboat, fore, aft and amidships, registered 116 degrees Fahrenheit as a maximum.

A second test was made, the boat being in the flames a total period of twenty-seven minutes. In that time a lifeboat of similar standard type could have travelled a distance of one-and-a-half miles from a burning ship. These tests convinced the Ministry of War Transport, and the converted wooden boats were approved. A great many were treated before the first steel boat was ready, and many a tankerman had cause for gratitude to Mr. John Lamb and his colleagues for their work and the risks they took to prove the efficiency of the invention."

That wood could be more resistant than steel in such circumstances may seem incredible, so that the line of thought which led to this development might be of interest.

My theory was that whilst at ordinary combustion temperatures wood would burn more quickly than steel, a wooden lifeboat would resist the intense heat produced by oil burning on water for a longer time than would a lifeboat made of sheet steel, the reason being that in the burning process, wood first becomes charred and the charred layer produced tends to insulate and protect the wood underneath, whereas with steel no such protective layer is formed and the metal is quickly reduced to a molten state.

The temperature of the fire around the boat when tested was never accurately recorded as the thermometers generally broke with the heat. All that is known is that it was higher than 2,400°F. Heat produced by oil burning on water is probably far greater than would be the case when burnt on land, due to the heat generated splitting the water into its two elements, hydrogen and oxygen, both of which combine readily with the carbon in the oil and burn with great intensity. Certain it is that the temperature was so high that sheet steel one-sixteenth of an inch thick burnt almost as readily as a piece of cardboard and much more readily than wood half-an-inch thick. Proof of this was obtained rather dramatically as disclosed later.

Before the tests began it was arranged that communication between those inside the boat and those outside should be by a

Fireproof lifeboat under test.

filled with pure air I was told what had happened. It appears that the man who had been chosen to work the hand pump had not been present at any of the previous tests and had no idea that oil floating on water could burn with such ferocity or produce such a loud noise. Having been told by his foreman, probably many times and with emphasis, that " the lives of those in the boat are in your hands," the good chap no doubt resolved that if it depended upon him everything would be all right. All he had to do — continuing his probable line of thought — was to keep the pump lever working to and fro at a steady rate ! This he doubtless did until the roaring flames obscured the boat and he became less conscious of what his duties were, or perhaps it is fairer to say that he became too conscious of the important part allocated to him. In any case, he began working the pump faster and faster, until the energy put into the lever was more than it could stand and it broke. The hot spot seen from the inside of the boat was, therefore, due to stoppage of water, but thanks to the prompt and effective action by those in charge of operations the fire was extinguished within a few seconds of the man yelling at the top of his voice and excitedly waving the broken lever above his head.

Proof of the fire-resisting qualities of the lifeboat came from an unexpected quarter. On one side of the static tank in which the tests were carried out was a wall about ten feet high. Children had access to the other side of the wall and by some means were able to reach the top, where they sat watching operations. During one of the preliminary tests a dozen or more were sitting there like a row of sparrows on a fence, chattering amongst themselves as children do and occasionally calling out to some of the men working at the tank. They were later joined by a little girl, who after getting herself firmly planted astride the wall asked the boy next to her, " What are they doing ? " This boy, about ten years old and probably the oldest, seized the opportunity to display his superior knowledge and replied, rather contempteously, "They're trying to burn that boat and they can't." There is no doubt that he was quite sure he could do so if given the opportunity.

CHAPTER XXI

TWO MEAT PIES WITH A DIFFERENCE

IT is with pride that I recall having, with very few exceptions, got on well with those with and for whom I have worked. One of the exceptions was a man who held a very high position. He was, in fact, a Director of one of the largest and most prosperous businesses in the world, and was considered very knowledgeable He must have been, because he later became a Cabinet Minister in his own country. He was a zealous patriot and was convinced that no country could produce better engineers and naval architects than his own. I admired him for his patriotism, but could not, of course, accept in silence his oft-repeated views that British technicians were only second best.

I had to work under him during the 1939-45 war. Although he didn't appeal to me any more than I apparently appealed to him, I tried hard to please, but after a time realised that it was a pretty hopeless task. Nevertheless, being subordinate it was my duty to continue trying, and I missed no opportunity to get on better terms.

I was therefore pleased when he asked me to accompany him to Glasgow, since there are worse ways for two people to get on good terms than by taking a long train journey together. However, just before the day of departure arrived he found that business engagements wouldn't allow him to travel by day, so sleeping berths were booked on the night train. This was unfortunate, as travelling in this way doesn't offer the same facilities for conversation. Moreover, after some minutes of not too difficult conversation, my companion said good-night and "turned-in." I cannot, therefore, claim an improvement in our relationship as a result of this journey to Glasgow together, but I can relate the following amusing story.

It was winter, and the most severe the country had seen for many years. Road and rail traffic were held up in some parts for days, owing to heavy falls of snow. A train was actually marooned for a week in a snow drift on one of the N.W. Scottish branch lines. Even in London the ice and frozen snow were thick and irregular enough to stop all traffic, including buses operating on certain main streets. No buses travelled along Baker Street for two days while Corporation employees melted the ice with fires on small wheeled bogeys.

An air raid was in progress over London when we left about 9 p.m. An hour or so later I " turned-in " as my travelling companion had already done so and there was nothing to watch. At that time the windows of trains were completely blacked-out and heavy penalties were imposed for merely lifting the corner of a blind to look out. Nobody did, because after dark there was nothing to see unless it was the flash from guns or exploding bombs.

The train stopped very frequently and ran slowly for long periods all through the night, due mainly, I was told later, to a heavy air raid on the Liverpool area. The result was that we did not crawl into Carlisle until 11 o'clock next morning, some four hours after the train was scheduled to arrive at Glasgow. At 8 o'clock we had been given a cup of tea and a couple of biscuits, so that long before reaching Carlisle most of us, including my travelling companion, felt very hungry. He complained bitterly about food not being put on the train to meet such an emergency, as would have been done in his own country no doubt! I thought his complaints unreasonable, but determined that if I could get him something to eat at Carlisle I would do so, as there was just a chance that it might soften his attitude towards me and my country. Also, of course, I was much in need of food myself!

I was one of the first off the train as it slowed down, and having previously located the station restaurant I made for it at the double. My prompt action, however, was of no avail, for I arrived to find not a thing to eat in the place. As I began to make my way back to the train I must have looked hungry as well as disappointed for a little soldier propping up one of the door posts said in almost a whisper "After something to eat ? " I nodded, and he then said, again so that no one else could hear, " I heard her (pointing in the direction of one of the waitresses) tell a laddie to fetch a tray of pies from somewhere." I said "Are you waiting for them ? " and he nodded in a way which meant " Yes." I therefore took up my stand at the other door post opposite my new found friend, both of us trying not to let others guess what we were waiting for.

After a few minutes the little soldier said excitedly " Here he comes," and as I looked in the direction in which he was facing, there sure enough, was a laddie carrying something before him that could be a tray of pies hidden under a cloth. The laddie was in no hurry though, and it seemed to take him ages to cover the thirty or forty yards to where I was standing, with money all ready in my hand.

At long last he was passing between the soldier and me and at that very moment the whistle blew, indicating the immediate departure of my train. As I was about to dart for the train the cloth over what the laddie was carrying was whisked off and there, behold, were about two dozen pies. Not stopping to think who had performed the conjuring trick so neatly, I threw my half-crown on the tray and grabbed a pie in each hand. The whole thing was done so quickly that I must have been well on the way towards my train before the laddie recovered from his astonishment.

By the time I reached the train it was gathering speed at much too great a rate for my liking, especially as neither of my hands was free. Just as I was about to throw away one of the ill-gotten pies so that I had a free hand to open the nearest carriage door, a porter seeing my predicament began to run with me. After a few more moments he managed to open a door and I prepared to board the train, still clutching a pie in each hand. At the same instant that I got a foot on the step something hit me pretty hard in the middle of the back and I went sprawling full length across the carriage gangway. As I lay face downwards I heard the door close with a bang and knew with some relief that I was safely on board, even though it was at the wrong end of the train.

I didn't rise from my recumbent and undignified position immediately, because in falling something dreadful had happened. The pie in my left hand was still there, even though it was so badly

I threw my half-crown on the tray and ran after my train.

crushed as to be almost unrecognisable, but the one which had been in my right hand was scattered in pieces of varying size all over the floor, which, being war-time, had not been washed for months, or maybe years, judging by the dirt on my clothes.

Meat pies at that time were things which money could not always buy, so the first thing I did was to pick up the pieces I could get hold of and put them in my clean handkerchief, the only article suitable for the purpose at hand. Then after removing some of the dirt from my clothes, I started off along the corridor to look for my sleeping berth, my intention upon arriving there being to wrap the pie which was badly crushed, but still in one piece, in paper for my boss and keep what remained of the other for myself.

Judging from the speed of the train it was evident that conditions on the track were much better North of Carlisle than they had been all night, and that the driver intended to make up some of the time lost. What with bruised and grazed limbs as a result of my unorthodox boarding of the train at Carlisle, both hands fully engaged protecting the pies from further damage and being jolted from one side of the corridor to the other, the length of that train seemed endless. I felt sure that another train had been hooked on at the last stop and that by the time I had found my berth I would have walked all the way to Glasgow!

When beginning to despair of ever reaching my berth I found myself in a first-class sleeping car. The realisation gave me renewed strength as I felt that I couldn't be far from my destination. When about half-way along the car a door of one of the sleeping berths opened and a woman stepped out, blocking my way. As she stood facing me she evidently wanted to go in the direction from which I came, but made no attempt to pass or to get out of my way by stepping back into her berth. I then noticed that her eyes were rivetted upon the crushed pie in my upturned hand. Her silence and refusal to make way for me suggested that the good lady could not believe her eyes. Then when the meeting was beginning to get embarrassing she cried "Pies! Where did you get them?" I told her and she then wailed "Oh! if I had only known, my little girl is famishing.

Being eager to please my boss, as well as feeling hungry myself, the mention of a little girl who was also hungry certainly put me in a dilemma, but only for a moment. Being an ex-seaman it was a case of putting into practice the axiom " women and children first," so the better of the two pies was handed over.

By the time I reached my sleeping berth I hadn't decided what to do with the remains of the other pie. I was quite prepared to eat it myself after I had carefully examined each piece, I was so hungry. On the other hand, it was only right that I should hand it over to my boss, even if he did think that I had eaten the better one and saved the worst for him. I therefore transferred the pieces from my handkerchief to paper and took them along to him. In handing over what remained of this pie I told him what had happened, omitting, of course, that I had gathered the pieces from the dirty floor of the carriage. As he didn't ask me to have any of the pieces I am sure I interpreted his thought correctly, so that it was with some satisfaction that I watched him eat the pieces of pie.

Never again did I begin a journey in war-time without a well-packed luncheon box and a vacuum flask filled with tea. More than once I had reason to be grateful to the hands that took so much care to ensure that I would not have an experience similar to the one just described. Although my packed luncheon was never called upon to keep me right with a difficult superior, it relieved the pangs of hunger of many people who travelled with me on various occasions during those trying war years when food was not easy to come by and the time taken to make long train journeys so uncertain.

CHAPTER XXII

BRIDGING A GAP

THERE came a time during the second world war when many of our ships sailing in convoy between the great oil port of Curacao in the Netherlands West Indies and the United Kingdom were being sunk with appalling loss of life. The attacks mostly occurred when the convoys were about half way across the Atlantic, and it was evident that the German submarines were concentrating their efforts at this part of the ocean.

There was ample evidence to show that the matter could be left to the British Navy, but as news of sinkings and still more sinkings came in I can be excused for thinking there might be something wrong with the method of convoying merchant ships, to the extent of working out a new method, which when completed was submitted by arrangement to several high Admiralty officials late one night in the early part of 1942. As might be expected, my proposal for giving better protection to convoys, produced from a limited knowledge of the situation, was politely but firmly turned down on the score of impracticability. However, when later discussing conditions at sea with the Masters of our ships, and the newest tactics employed in convoy, I thought I recognised bits of my proposal, but this was probably just imagination !

With, perhaps, a view to alleviating the disappointment I felt at my efforts being in vain, I was told in strict confidence that the cause of so many sinkings about mid-Atlantic was not any deficiency in the method of convoying, but lack of air cover. The official view was that the only solution to this serious problem was more aircraft carriers, but unfortunately such ships were not available and could not be built under three years.

Aircraft patrols were operating from each side of the Atlantic but their fuel range was such that a gap about five hundred miles wide remained unpatrolled. One method of defending this gap in our defences had already been tried by the British Admiralty and Air Force. It comprised Hurricane fighters carried on specially equipped merchant ships, the aircraft being catapulted from launching ways on the ships' decks. Their main purpose, however, was interception of enemy dive bombers as convoys approached the U.K., rather than the driving off of submarines.

The weakness of this form of defence against submarines when applied about mid-Atlantic, was that if the aircraft crew could not reach land subsequently, they had to bale out and take to an inflated rubber dinghy carried by all such aircraft. Thus a valuable aeroplane was lost and the crew placed in considerable danger. Many brave men lost their lives in this way. This noble service was operated by pilots of what was called the Merchant Service Fighter Unit of the R.A.F., but all their valour could not compensate for the shortage of ships with facilities which would enable the aircraft to fly off and return to them at the end of their patrol.

Our shipbuilding yards and engineering works were working to maximum capacity on a wide variety of ships ; destroyers for the destruction of submarines, and merchant ships to replace those sunk, not to mention cruisers and battleships to deal with enemy surface raiders that might slip out into the Atlantic and beyond. It was, therefore, well nigh impossible to lay down new keels for aircraft carriers and complete them in time to stop the destruction of our merchant ships.

At this period all merchant ships were equipped with defensive armament, and when in convoy were escorted by warships of the small fast type. The only other protection that could be given was, therefore, air cover, and the only alternative to orthodox aircraft carriers was to convert, if possible, some existing ships into aircraft carriers.

Having got the idea that of all types of merchant ships the oil tanker was the most suitable, I and my staff feverishly began working out designs and soon decided that our 12,000 tons dead-weight ships, although rather small, could be quickly converted. They would provide a runway 460 feet long, which I was assured by an authority would be just sufficient for flying off. The same applied to landing, providing particular attention was given to the gear that would be necessary to arrest the speed of the aircraft as they touched down.

It is perhaps not surprising that the Admiralty also thought to provide the much needed air cover in this way and were at the same time working on plans to convert merchant ships, but of the general cargo type. I did not learn of their intentions until my plans were well advanced, but it gave me great satisfaction to know that they were prepared to consider using merchant ships for this purpose, as then they would doubtless give favourable consideration to my idea. I therefore lost no time in submitting my roughly unfinished plans to convert oil tankers into aircraft carriers, and at the meeting which was called, pointed out that whereas every general cargo ship converted would mean one ship less to transport much needed cargo, owing to the flight deck making it impossible to use cargo winches, an oil tanker could be fitted with a flight deck over her cargo space and still carry petroleum cargoes.

The advantage of obtaining aircraft carriers quickly without losing cargo space was fully appreciated, and many hours were spent by myself and about a dozen officials of the Admiralty and Ministry of War Transport discussing the matter from every conceivable angle. All were so eager to find a satisfactory solution to this most serious problem that I don't think any had previously gone so long without food. The meeting terminated an hour or so before midnight and, sad to relate, I left having failed to convince its members that it would not only be possible, but quite safe for fighter aircraft to take-off and land on a flight deck situated over 12,000 tons of inflammable petroleum. One of their objections was that, on landing an aircraft might crash through the thin flight deck and set the ship on fire, when, apart from the loss of the ship and valuable lives, the resulting smoke and flames would act as a beacon for prowling submarines. My proposals to prevent this happening were unacceptable and it was apparent that nothing would be gained by pursuing the matter further that day.

I left the building in which the meeting took place and walked into one of the worst London fogs I have ever experienced. Before leaving the building my spirits seemed to be as low as they could be, but when I saw the conditions under which I had to get home,

Oil Tanker "RAPANA" before and after conversion to
Aircraft Carrier.

my feelings can be left to the imagination. That was one occasion, however, when fog was not altogether unwelcome because it had stopped the bombing and silenced the anti-aircraft guns, for which respite all Londoners were, I'm sure, grateful.

Not knowing quite what I was doing, I turned into a little pub which I knew to be within a few yards of me and ordered a whisky and soda. Being the only customer, the young lady behind the counter soon put my order in front of me. Looking at it I said, " But this is a 'double' ". She replied, " I know, and it looks as if you need it." I had just finished arguing and was not prepared to start again, so I drank my first double whisky with the silent barmaid's eyes fixed upon me. Had she known that I had had nothing since breakfast but black coffee and biscuits, she might not have pressed me to do this rather unwise thing.

After not more than five minutes I left, to find the fog so thick that all traffic was at a standstill and impossible to see others afoot until colliding with them. My immediate destination was Trafalgar Square Tube Station. The double whisky had not robbed me of my sense of direction as I feared it might, and I felt confident that I would arrive safely providing I could keep to the footpaths I knew so well. Progress was naturally very slow as I had to guide myself by feeling the fronts of shops with my hand and scrape my feet to avoid stumbling over a kerb.

Groping my way along, I presently came into contact with a large obstacle across my path. After a moment's reflection I realised that it was a bus. " Now," thought I, " when did I leave the pavement and get on to the road ? I must try to remember otherwise I will lose my sense of direction and never reach Trafalgar Square until the fog lifts. Had that double whisky made me step off the pavement without realising that I had done so or was the bus really there ? " Before I could give the answers to these questions a voice near me said " Where do you want to be mate ? " I said that I wanted to get back to the pavement, to which he replied " You are on the pavement and so is this bus." This knowledge came as a great relief as I then knew that I still had control of my faculties. The owner of the voice then guided me around the bus and started me off in the direction of my destination, which I reached without further incident.

The ravages of the enemy submarines operating in packs about mid-Atlantic continued, and so acute did the situation become that in September 1942 I was requested to again submit with the least possible delay my scheme to convert oil tankers into aircraft carriers. All preliminary plans for the now famous M.A.C. (Merchant Aircraft Carriers) ships were prepared in record time by the Marine Technical Division of The Anglo-Saxon Petroleum Company under my direction. With very few modifications they were quickly accepted by the Admiralty and Ministry of War Transport, and the none too easy task of arranging for nine selected oil tankers to arrive at United Kingdom ports precisely when needed began. Before each ship arrived, over 800 tons of steel had to be fabricated and made ready to be erected in proper sequence, and so avoid the job taking a day longer than was necessary.

The first on the list was the motor ship *Rapana*. She arrived at the North Shields ship repair yard of Smith's Dock Co., Ltd. in February 1943 and emerged in her new guise five months later, forerunner of a flotilla destined to play an important role in defeating the object of German submarines. Ships of the same class were chosen because the conversion work could be simplified and speeded up by the use of standardised parts. A similar ship building at the time was also converted, to bring the total number of M.A.C. ships to ten.

The conversion of these ten tankers into aircraft carriers by our ship repairing yards in twenty-one months was a remarkable achievement, particularly as they were already busily engaged making good an endless procession of badly war-damaged ships of all kinds. A further reason for satisfaction was that the usefulness of these ships as cargo carriers was impaired only to a small degree, their individual capacity being reduced from 12,000 to 11,000 tons and their speed from 12 to $11\frac{1}{2}$ knots, while their behaviour in adverse weather came up to highest expectations.

In preparing the many necessary plans for the conversion of oil tankers to aircraft carriers a series of intricate technical difficulties had to be overcome. For instance, part of the amidships accom-

You are on the pavement, and so is this bus.

modation, the navigating bridge, the upper structure at the after end of the ship and, of course, the 30 foot high funnel, had to be cut down. This was to allow the flight deck, which was to extend over the entire length and breadth of the ship, to be situated low enough to ensure the necessary solidarity, and avoid the added top weight adversely affecting the stability of the ship. Also, to provide for changes in temperature between hot and cold climates and for flexing of the ship in a seaway, the flight deck had to be constructed in a way which would allow it to expand and contract freely. In the class of ship selected, the hogging and sagging in a rough sea amounted to about four inches.

The naval aircraft carrier is designed with horizontal funnels, exhausts would be a better description. These are situated well aft on both sides of the hull, and a system of water sprays damps down the smoke and gases that might otherwise swirl over the ship and prove a danger to an air pilot coming in to alight. An equally ingenious system was introduced to replace the oil tanker's funnel, and a further feature of the conversion was a neat structure on the starboard side that combined navigation bridge, aircraft control platform and signal-top.

A redistribution and increase of armamemt had to be made. The orthodox four-inch stern gun was housed under the flight-deck aft, and steel sponsons were built out on either side of the flight-deck to support the dual-purpose guns — two Bofors and six Oerlikons. Another structural problem solved successfully was the provision of accommodation for nearly double the number of personnel normally borne in a tanker. The additional complement were mostly officers and men of the Fleet Air Arm of the Royal Navy, and the increase necessitated extra space for galleys, bakeries and a sick bay complete, in the naval style, with a well-equipped operating theatre for casualties.

All-British crews were engaged, and officers had to take a short, intensive course of special training before commissioning. They had to become accustomed, for instance, to navigating from the diminutive bridge on the starboard side, which invariably proved awkward at first. They also had to become accustomed to finding their way about the deck among the innumerable criss-cross girders supporting the flight-deck overhead, where at first you had the impression of wandering in the maze of a gigantic Meccano set.

The advent of the M.A.C. ship caused both the naval authorities and the shipowners to be apprehensive about the inclusion of equal numbers of men of the Royal Navy and the Merchant Navy in a hybrid ship commanded by a Merchant Navy Master. Some anticipated dissension, for it was the first time that personnel of the Fleet Air Arm and the Merchant Navy had been called upon to work in such intimate co-operation. But fears of any rivalry or jealousy were quickly dispelled. Contacts were cordial from the first.

The enlarged complement drawn from the two Services proved an advantage in more ways than one. Social life, which is limited in an oil tanker, blossomed under the changed conditions prevalent in a M.A.C. ship. The spacious flight-deck could be transformed in port into a " recreational field," in a manner impossible with an oil tanker's deck, encumbered as it is by numerous hatches and other obstacles.

Deck hockey became a popular sport, and matches between teams representative of the seamen and airmen were arranged. When opportunity was afforded by a stay in port, a combined team would be selected and a challenge issued to other ships, the keenest enthusiasm being shown for matches between M.A.C. ships of the Shell Group. While the high open deck of the new type escort provided facility for this and other sports, the size and variety of the ship's complement, amounting to 115 officers and men of the two Services, gave encouragement to such "indoor" social activities as competitive games, the Brains Trust, Quiz and Discussion Groups.

The air staff of the oil tankers converted to Merchant Aircraft Carriers consisted, in the main, of pilots, air-gunners, observers and maintenance men, and extra naval gunners were appointed to man the ships' additional armament. The aircraft carried were three to five Swordfish biplanes, and these was lashed snugly at the after end of the flight-deck when not in use, since no provision could be made for hydraulic lifts and below-deck hangers, as in a naval aircraft carrier.

Sometimes more than one M.A.C. ship would be included in one of the large convoys on the regular northern route between Halifax, Nova Scotia, and the Clyde. Their planes would afford protection by aerial reconnaissance, usually making a dawn, midday and dusk patrol in search of any submarines that might be in the vicinity. These scouts could also be highly offensive. Each Swordfish was armed with two depth-charges and four small bombs, or, alternatively, with rockets of great destructive power. It was claimed that a rocket-shell would penetrate right through a surfaced submarine, and, indeed, several hostile submarines were destroyed in this way during the latter part of the war.

Patrols were arranged by the S.O.E. — the Senior Officer of the Escort. He was the unwilling cause of the Shipmaster losing a good deal of sleep in the course of a voyage. Whenever he deemed it advisable, he would request a patrol, at any time of the day or night, and the Master of the M.A.C. ship would immediately call his Air Staff Officer (an R.N. or R.N.V.R. Lieutenant-Commander) into conference. The pair would confer on the request with special regard to weather conditions, and if agreeable to it, would signal the S.O.E. to inform him how many planes they would fly.

The new-type aircraft carrier had a flight-deck 460 by 60 feet, which gave a small margin for error in taking-off and alighting in unfavourable weather conditions. Seen from a height by the returning pilot the flight-deck looked about the size of a floating matchbox, and, indeed, good judgement was needed by him and the controlling officer aboard the ship — invariably known as " Bats " from the shape of his signalling apparatus — to effect a safe landing on a none-too-spacious deck of a rolling, pitching ship. Nevertheless, the usual kind of mishap was nothing worse than an undignified encounter with the crash-barrier if a plane did not bring up smartly on the arrester-wires stretched athwart the deck.

For a lengthy voyage a destroyer or corvette would need " topping-up " with fuel oil, and on many occasions the M.A.C. assumed the role of parent-ship. A thirty-fathom line with a buoy attached would be paid out from the stern, and the escort would glide into the M.A.C. ship's wake to pick it up with a grapnel. By means of the line the naval craft could haul in the end of the oil hose, through which the fuel oil would be pumped while the two ships steamed on parallel courses at normal convoy speed.

When the end of the war came, all ten M.A.C. ships were still afloat and doing useful work. Some were damaged and put out of commission, but not for long. Within twelve months of the end of hostilities all had been returned to their original form and are still (1954) doing the work for which they were originally constructed.

CHAPTER XXIII

THE MIGHT OF A SPARK

MANY ships were badly battered during the second world war by a ruthless enemy. To describe a portion only of those with which I alone had to deal would require too much space and would not all be pleasant reading even now. The *Liseta* incident, however, was rather different. She was badly battered, but not by a malicious enemy ; the damage was so extensive that had it occurred at sea she would have sunk in the matter of minutes and a most interesting job would have been denied me. Moreover, I would not have been able to relate this narrative.

Of 3,600 tons carrying capacity and rather small as ships go these days, the Royal Dutch Shell oil tanker *Liseta* was nevertheless one that could ill be spared. Built in the year 1927 when another world war was furthest from the minds of those who built her, she began her career peacefully enough in distant parts, but when in 1941 the call went out for little ships to distribute aviation spirit around the submarine infested waters and aircraft haunted skies of the United Kingdom, the *Liseta*, together with four others of her size, at once answered the call.

With very little preparation these five small oil tankers left the Caribbean Sea and began the 3,000 mile voyage across the Atlantic, bringing with them much needed petroleum. Of the five ships that set out in this perilous journey, three only got safely through, the *Liseta* being one of them. The unfortunate ones were the victims of preying submarines, and only some of the gallant seamen lived to tell of their adventure.

During thirty-three months' trading between various ports in the U.K. the *Liseta* had many exciting experiences with enemy submarines and aircraft, but torpedoes and bombs did not stop the work of vital national importance assigned to her. Then one day, after discharging another cargo of aviation spirit at Preston in Lancashire, and before the highly explosive gases remaining in her cargo tanks could be expelled, prior to proceeding to sea in accordance with custom, a tiny spark, probably no bigger than is sometimes seen to fall from the end of a cigarette, found its way to a vital part. In an instant more damage was done by an explosion than could have resulted from a direct hit by bomb or torpedo.

Lying there, no longer floating, heeled over to an angle of twenty-five degrees, almost submerged, with practically the whole length of her decks ripped open to reveal the inner fabric of the ship, she was indeed a pitiful sight. It seemed incredible that a tiny spark had in an instant of time wrought such havoc, but there it was, and at first sight it appeared certain that the *Liseta's* contribution to the war effort was at an end.

The explosion was so violent that it was heard many miles away, the windows of buildings a quarter-of-a-mile off were smashed and parts which had been secured to the deck, such as the spare propeller weighing about one-and-a-half tons, were hurled a distance of 500 yards. The Master and five members of the crew who were on deck at the time were killed outright. Fire immediately followed the explosion, but courageous souls and willing hands soon had the fire under control.

The risk taken by those who fought the fire was great indeed, since parts of the ship still contained explosive gas. This was disclosed when the small portion of the deck still remaining intact, and on which the fire fighters were standing, suddenly lifted quite three feet due to a further explosion in the compartment underneath. Fortunately the composition of the gas in this compartment must have been near one end of the explosive range, otherwise the men would have been blown sky-high and the tragic death roll increased.

Occupying an important berth in a busy harbour, it was essential for the " remains " to be removed without delay. Owing to her badly damaged condition this involved great difficulties, but the matter was taken in hand by ship salvage experts who soon found that if the water inside the perforated hull could be pumped out at the rate of 2,500 tons an hour, or a little faster than the water ran in, the sunken wreck could be lifted just clear of the dock bottom, and it would be possible to drag her to a position where she would not interfere with the use of the port. The success of this operation depended, of course, upon the reliability of the salvage boat's pumps, since had these failed the *Liseta* would have rapidly filled and sunk in deeper water, where she would have been an even greater obstruction. Moreover, she could then have been removed only after complete dissection under water, a long, difficult and costly operation, during which the business of the port would have been seriously curtailed.

All arrangements having been made, the *Liseta* was floated clear of the dock bottom and moved out of the dock into the river by sturdy tugs. After two anxious hours she was safely moored to the north bank in such a position that ships could freely pass to and fro. At low water the *Liseta* was high and dry as the river was tidal, whilst at high water the internal spaces quickly filled and she became submerged. This completed the work of the salvage experts.

At each low tide the stricken *Liseta* sank deeper and deeper into the soft mud of the river bed, and as some mud found its way through the countless holes in the deformed hull each time the water receded she would eventually have become buried, and this particular spot would have been her last resting place. It was apparent that if anything could be done to save what was left of the good ship, it would have to be done quickly. This involved not only finding means of making her floatable, but in addition making her capable of being towed a distance of forty miles, fifteen of which would be in the open sea, to Birkenhead where facilities for carrying out the necessary repairs were available.

With a view to making her floatable my first idea was to stop all leaks in the hull by means of wooden plugs and quick-drying cement. This, however, proved impracticable owing to the thousands of openings requiring to be plugged and the difficulty of reaching many of them without first cutting away large portions of the tangled internal structures. To make matters worse, the contour of the river bed was such that at each low tide the ship made harder contact at mid-length than at the ends, consequently the strains set up in the weakened hull due to the overhanging ends caused cracks to appear in the upper plates, or, in other

The S/S "LISETA" after the explosion.

words, the ship began to break her back. Time, therefore, was a very important factor.

My next idea was to fill the inside of the damaged hull with empty, air-tight, forty-gallon oil drums. Calculations indicated that two thousand such drums would be required, an order not easily fulfilled. As soon as the details of the scheme could be worked out and the drums began arriving from all over the country, a start was made to pack them into position.

The buoyancy of these drums when submerged some twenty feet is very great, and it was necessary to secure them in place in such a way that the upward force exerted would have the desired result without imposing serious strains on the greatly weakened hull. The drums were therefore deposited at each low tide in predetermined positions. After a fortnight's hard work the ship was made floatable, but the distribution of the lifting forces was not just right and it was necessary to undo much of the good work and allow the ship to sink again. The soundness of the idea, however, had been proved.

A fresh start was made and this time the efforts of the ten men engaged on the job proved successful, the ship not only being made to float at high water, but upright and on an even keel, a trim which was considered necessary for the intended voyage to the repair port.

The disposition of the drums, by reason of the location of the heaviest damage, had perforce to be such that the ends of the ship received most of their support, and whilst the ship was now safe enough in placid waters, there was a possibility that she would break in two and sink, if when the open sea was reached it was less placid. To provide the necessary longitudinal strength, a long and deep girder, surmounted by a heavy rider-plate, was welded to the narrow remaining strips of deck on each side of the ship, and cross lashings of stout wire stretched between them. With the limited facilities available at Preston, difficulties were encountered in dealing with these heavy structures, but they were overcome and once again the *Liseta* had a backbone.

As the ship was still resting on the uneven river bed at low tides and being subjected to strains which caused the cracks in the hull plating to extend, and as the drydock at Birkenhead would not be vacant for ten days, permission to move the *Liseta* into a non-tidal berth where she would float constantly was given by the Preston Harbour Authorities, who, I must admit, were not easily persuaded that she would remain afloat and cause them no further anxiety. The operation was carried out without incident in ideal weather for the job, and to my great relief she remained afloat without appreciable alteration in draught.

The thoughts of those on the job, however, would persist in turning to the drums in the bowels of the ship, which were exposed to the greatest external pressure. Had they collapsed under the pressure it would not have been surprising, because having to be procured at very short notice many of them had done service in the manner intended and did not look capable of supporting their own weight, let alone 1,116 tons, which was the weight of the *Liseta* as she lay in the water.

The final preparations for the voyage to Birkenhead included devising the safest method of securing the towing hawsers, as owing to the weak state of the hull it was too risky to tow in the ordinary way. The method adopted was to encircle the ship with a single towing hawser in such a way that the ship would be pulled from the stern, and so reduce to a minimum the strains set up at mid-length where she was already splitting into two parts.

The stage was all set at noon on the day the drydock became vacant, the high water mark being reached about three o'clock in the afternoon. A smooth sea was required before the voyage could be undertaken if the certainty of the ship foundering on the way was to be avoided. Weather reports received from various sources during the morning were rather conflicting, and it was not until first-hand information was received from an incoming ship that the decision was made to abandon the attempt that day. This delay was unfortunate because it was considered desirable to complete the journey in daylight, and each day's delay meant a later start owing to high water mark being progressively later.

Being war-time, no weather reports were broadcast by wireless, so that local reports had to be relied upon. These were eagerly sought, and by noon the following day the prospects of favourable weather were good and all last minute preparations were made to begin the voyage at dead high water, which was 3.30 p.m.

The ship was then lying in a small enclosed dock called a wet basin, and to reach the river Ribble had to pass through narrow lock gates. Owing to the fragile condition of the *Liseta* the tugs did not find this an easy task. The operation, however, was successfully accomplished and a start was made to move down the river, a distance of twelve miles before reaching the open sea.

The *Liseta* was deformed and twisted so badly that it was almost impossible to keep her moving on a straight course. The voyage was begun by having two tugs ahead and two tugs astern, but immediately upon getting under way the *Liseta* darted for the North bank. The Skipper of the tug on the South side quickly endeavoured to turn her bow into mid-stream, much to the concern of us on board who knew more about the weakened condition of the ship than did the tugboat Skipper. The action of of the tug brought the *Liseta's* bow towards mid-stream quickly enough, but unfortunately the swing continued and she then charged for the opposite bank. This erratic behaviour continued nearly all the way down the river and on several occasions the river banks were touched, but fortunately the ship did not stick.

Various tug dispositions were tried with the object of keeping the ship more or less in mid-stream, but it was not until the first half of the twelve miles had been covered that it was found that the best control could be exercised by having three tugs ahead and one astern. Of the three tugs ahead, one took up a position on the Port bow, another on the Starboard bow and the third directly ahead, the tugs on each bow maintaining taut their short towing wires, the ahead tug alone being responsible for progress.

The open sea was reached about 7 p.m., and by that time the N.W. wind had freshened. In ordinary circumstances the sea would have been considered calm, but where freeboard (distance from sea level to deck) was only three inches and inside the ship were hundreds of tons of uncontrollable water which moved like a tidal wave from side to side as the ship rolled, the slightest movement gave cause for anxiety. Moreover, there could be no turning back, as by that time the tide had receded too far to permit doing so.

At this stage two of the four tugs cast off and returned home, since even in such precarious undertakings, economy must be considered. The two remaining tugs then took up stations, one a long distance ahead and the other an equal distance astern in order to minimise the risk of putting strain on the *Liseta*. As she heaved and rolled she groaned as though each movement caused her great pain, but nevertheless good progress was made, that is if two miles an hour is considered a good speed, which it certainly was in the circumstances.

Owing to so much time being lost in leaving the berth and navigating the river it soon became apparent that we would not arrive before the Port of Liverpool was closed, an hour after sunset, and that the voyage would have to be completed next morning. Therefore, when darkness fell it was decided to stop until dawn, as not only would moving so near the unlighted coast entail risks, but there was no point in arriving off the river where the drydock was situated before the procession would be allowed to enter.

No anchors being available, it was necessary for one tug to hold on to the *Liseta* all night and so prevent her drifting ashore. The night was very dark, with occasional gusts of wind and flurries of rain. No lights were permissible either on the *Liseta* or the tugs. so that the task of the tug assigned the duty of steaming slowly round the ship and her "anchor" tug was not an easy one as they had to be constantly on the alert. But the vigil of the five of us on the *Liseta* was lightened by the occasional sound of the circling tug as we listened to the groans of fractured plates and the snapping of rivets as the ship rolled uneasily to the swell. It needed no vivid imagination to realise that as each rivet snapped the *Liseta* was further weakened at some vital point, and that the next one to go might be the signal to jump into the rowing boat lying alongside and hope to get clear before the ship sank.

The break of dawn was anxiously looked for and greatly welcomed when it came, and no time was lost in re-connecting the second tug, which again took up a position astern, and resuming the journey. The weather had not improved during the night nor had it deteriorated, which was something to be very

We listened to the groans of fractured plates and the
snapping of rivets.

thankful for.

In spite of every precaution being taken a few mishaps occurred during this short but adventurous voyage. On one occasion the towing hawser broke and owing to there being no mechanical power on board the *Liseta* herculean efforts were needed to connect up with a new hawser. On another occasion a towing hawser fouled the propeller of one of the tugs, and things looked very black until superb handling got it clear.

When the mouth of the river Mersey came in sight the decks, or what remained of them, were level with the sea, but the ship was at last in smooth water. It was then felt that all troubles were over, but further danger approached from an unexpected quarter. This was due to the curiosity aroused on board overtaking ships, since all they could see was two ends of something above water being towed by a powerful tug. In spite of warnings these overtaking ships approached so closely that the bow waves made by them rolled over the *Liseta*. This occurred time and again, so that it was a great relief on arriving at our destination to find the drydock gates open and officials and workmen of Cammell Laird & Co., Ltd. ready to do everything possible to assist the *Liseta* into drydock.

Four months later the good ship was completely restored, and when the end of the war came was still making her important contribution.

CHAPTER XXIV

MY WAR YEARS IN LONDON

BEING in London throughout the whole of the second world war, excepting for a few months in 1940, I saw much of the ruthless bombing of that great city by screeching high explosives, hideous land mines, noisy V.1s and finally the silent V.2s. At times it seemed as though few of us would see the next dawn, and that those who did would find London a heap of ruins. It was not until later that I realised how well and truly had London been built.

When in May 1940 I returned to my old Company, they, like all businesses able to do so, had been evacuated. The department for which I was made responsible had gone to Plymouth and for the first few weeks I also operated from that fine historic city. Very soon, however, I found that I had been appointed to so many Admiralty and Ministry of War Transport committees that too much of my time was being spent travelling to London. Consequently London became my headquarters, and for a time my secretary, Miss Curchin, the firewatchers and I were the sole occupants of St. Helen's Court, which normally accommodated a staff of about one thousand.

The bombing about this time wasn't severe, it taking place after dark and not every night. Sometimes we were left in peace for several nights in succession. As time went by my committments became heavier and I found it impossible to visit Plymouth as often as I wished. It was then that I arranged for a number of my staff to return to London. But no sooner had they got nicely settled at St. Helen's Court than the Germans started day as well as night bombing.

This seriously interfered with the work, as my Principals had decreed that as soon as a warning was given, all except the firewatchers must proceed to the bomb-proof basement and remain there until the " all clear " had been sounded. Many were the times when the staff would just reach their desks and another

" alarm " would be given. It got so bad, in fact, that the question of re-evacuating was considered, but by that time most of the staff had become hardened to this new form of warfare and, with few exceptions, wished to remain in London and face up to the dangers and discomforts.

It was about this time that I left London on a secret Government mission. When I returned some six months later, my mission completed, round-the-clock bombing of London was getting well under way, and to work or sleep, the only two things the few people in London at that time thought about, was far from easy. The work did go on, however, even though on many a night sleep was impossible, and upon looking back, one cannot help but marvel at what was achieved. Two outstanding qualities in the British character saved the situation, namely, the increasing desire to hit back as matters became worse, and the capacity to gather strength from humorous remarks made by people in all walks of life under the most trying conditions imaginable.

Surprising as it may seem, there was plenty to be seen and heard to keep up one's spirits. Some of the things heard were really funny, while some of the things seen, apart from war damage, were most unusual. For instance, London bus drivers, being in my opinion the best in the world, never in normal times get themselves into a position where they must go backwards, not even in the densest London traffic, which cannot be more dense in any part of the world.

The only time I saw such an unusual sight was whilst a passenger in a bus going along Baker Street towards Oxford Street. It was fairly early one morning and I was on my way to catch a main line train. The German bombers were overhead but out of sight, and the noise of our anti-aircraft guns was deafening. Suddenly a cloud of dust was seen to rise about five hundred yards ahead and a moment later the bus, which was standing, was struck by the blast and pushed backwards several yards.

We in the bus felt nothing, and whilst we were wondering if the driver was all right, he turned round in his seat to see what was happening at the rear, whereupon the conductress, who was quite unperturbed, rang the bell and the bus proceeded slowly on its way. The cloud of dust ahead didn't clear as quickly as the bus driver expected, due probably to the atmospheric conditions prevailing at the time, and he decided to take another route. It was then that I saw for the first time, and never since, a London bus driven backwards for several hundred yards.

A few days afterwards I had occasion to be walking in the vicinity of this incident. I knew, of course, that a bomb had fallen thereabouts but I didn't expect to find a hole extending almost the full width of the street and quite thirty feet deep. As far as I could judge, that bus must have been stopped about fifty yards from the crater.

This was happening all over London at that time, and as a Northerner I raise my hat to Londoners for their total disregard of danger and determination to get on with their jobs. Train services were disrupted and on many occasions a journey that would normally take an hour took three or four hours, but the passengers invariably got to their city offices in good spirits, even if they arrived to find no gas, electricity or water available and nothing much to eat. I will never forget seeing a number of young women, in their delicate shoes and looking as natty as ever, scrambling over a huge heap of rubble near the Bank Underground station, where just a few hours previously nearly four hundred people, sleeping in the station for safety, had been killed by a direct hit on the station. These girls could have avoided the rubble by taking a round-about course, but the one they selected was the quickest and would get them to their desks in the shortest time.

The department of the Anglo-Saxon Petroleum Company for which I was then responsible was divided into three sections, the New Construction Section, the Repairs and Maintenance Section and the Nautical Section, in charge of Mr. Rigg, Mr. Youldon and Captain Loos respectively, all of long and varied experience in the construction and operation of oil tankers. All had reached retiring age soon after war broke out but readily agreed to remain at their posts until the dreadful business was over. Although I was much younger and had served under all of them at different times, their loyalty and valuable help is a memory I shall always cherish.

I was also fortunate in those immediately around me. There was Miss Curchin, my private secretary, Miss Hall and Miss Adlam her assistants, and Mr. J. G. Robinson, my personal technical assistant. Dorothy Curchin, daughter of a well known naval architect, average in height and build, brown hair, face that would inspire confidence, fearless of bombs, energy unlimited, was the essence of efficiency and industry. She wasn't above polishing furniture in my office if the charwoman disappointed, making tea, scouring the city for cigarettes or anything else I wanted, while come what may she was always there. Never a day passed but my desk was adorned with flowers. Where and how she got them at such times will always be a mystery to me.

Miss Curchin's assistants had both been given the name Patricia. We called them Big Pat and Little Pat, just why I cannot explain, as they were both about the same height. Miss Hall was a little older and not quite so slim, which perhaps accounts for the distinction. Both were nice girls and devoted to Miss Curchin and myself.

Mr. Robinson was referred to as " Little Robbie " because he was small in stature and to distinguish him from another Robinson in the department who was older and taller. None could be more willing nor more reliable than Little Robbie. He seemed to take a delight in working by day and travelling by night, while I could be sure that anything which interested me would have his interest also.

Our building had the attention of the German bombers three times. On the first occasion a five-hundred pound high explosive left the sixth and seventh floors a mass of debris and killed one of our firewatchers. On the second occasion, five incendiary bombs landed on the roof — or where the roof had been — but were fortunately extinguished before they could set fire to the building. On the last occasion an oil bomb fell on the top of the building but didn't ignite. The bomb, however, which resembled a large oil drum, rolled to the fifth floor entrance of the lift shaft and stuck there. Had it fallen down the shaft, as it easily could have done, the gate being open, St. Helen's Court would have suffered the same fate as a similar building within a hundred yards of it. The spot where this building once stood has been levelled and is now a large improvised car park.

I frequently visited Billiter Buildings, in which Trewent & Proctor's offices were situated, to discuss matters of mutual interest with my old friend Johnny Horton. Usually I called in the morning on the way to my own office, the two offices being only about five minutes' walking distance apart.

One morning I arrived to find the main entrance to Billiter Buildings, and the building adjoining one end of it, a heap of rubble. A cloud of dust was still hanging over the place where the building had been some four hours before. Going round to the back entrance I eventually reached Trewent & Proctor's office to find the four rooms in a frightful state and my little friend standing, with tears in his eyes, looking at the place where he had worked for over fifty years. One of the rooms was open to the outside air, while ceilings of the others were down, windows had gone, every piece of furniture except the heaviest was out of its customary place and all covered with lime and lumps of masonry.

The railway by which I normally travelled between the City and my flat, the Metropolitan, was put out of action for over two years by a chance bomb. The alternative route was between Marble Arch and the Bank on the Central Line. This line is situated at such a depth that there was a possibility of it being flooded from the river Thames, so that until water-tight doors had been fitted the stations were closed during air raids, and I and other travellers had to find our way to work as best we could. Fortunately the buses never stopped running, although it was not always certain that they would complete their scheduled journey, in which event the journey had to be completed on foot unless one was lucky enough to get a taxi or a lift on a passing lorry. In my journeys to and fro I saw many gruesome sights which are best forgotten.

After a time things got rather too hot in the vicinity of my flat, and because of this and the hazards and uncertainties of the journey to and from the city I decided to go into an hotel, and chose the Norman Hotel on the Thames Embankment. Arriving

N

about eight o'clock one evening I had a meal of sorts and then strolled into the lounge, where there were about a dozen people. The bombs were coming down thick and fast, and I shall never forget pausing in the doorway and being amused by a party of five foreigners at a table in one of the inner corners of the room. I think they were German refugees, who whenever they heard a bomb on the way literally dived under an Anderson table shelter, to which they evidently considered they had priority. After the bomb landed they would emerge very cautiously one at a time, and what made it really funny was that sometimes they would hear another bomb on its way before they reached an upright position and would again dive under the table. Some of them were so fat that their agility, or lack of it, had to be seen to be fully appreciated.

The hotel manager would not let us sleep in our rooms that night because he said it was far too dangerous. The fact was that he had had beds erected in the basement, and the rooms had been stripped of all moveable articles and stowed in some supposedly safe place. The beds in the basement were rows of crude wooden bunks. They were fairly comfortable but I paid my bill and left the next morning, as I couldn't endure another night in such a smelly atmosphere and be kept awake by the grunts and groans of the sleepers who were evidently more accustomed to such an atmosphere. On that night the beautiful little church of St. Clements Dane in the middle of the Strand, where it had stood for well over 200 years, received a direct hit, and two men near the Norman Hotel at the time were killed by blast. One of the victims was, I believe, the night porter.

The basement of St. Helen's Court had been fitted out as an air-raid shelter and First Aid Post, and after my short experience of hotel life I decided to spend my nights there in future. The large basement had been so well strengthened that it was proof against anything the Germans could drop, and although bombs could be felt when they landed within the city walls, we were spared the noise of the anti-aircraft gunfire. With a camp bed and blankets and means of providing myself with a nice strong cup of tea whenever I wanted it, I soon settled in.

The advantage of sleeping and working in the same building was the time saved in travelling. This gave me so much more time for work that without realising it I found that my working day had extended somewhat. Actually it was from 6 a.m. to 11 p.m. with, of course, breaks for meals. The solutions to many problems were worked out about this time, such as the safe carriage of all sorts of war material on the decks of oil tankers, the conversion of ships for the landing of troops and equipment on enemy territory, the design of fast tankers for fuelling the fleet whilst at sea, drawing up plans for getting badly damaged ships to repair ports, working out all sorts of ideas for turning tankers round in port in the shortest possible time and so increasing the quantity of vital petroleum imported, designing small petrol carriers for river and coastal service during the recapture of Burma and other countries occupied by the enemy, and a hundred and one other jobs necessary for the successful prosecution of the war.

Designing the small petrol carriers for river and coastal service in the East was a particularly interesting job. Each of these craft, of which a large number were built, carried about 300 tons of motor spirit. They were constructed in such a way that they could be dismantled afloat and lifted on to the deck of a deep sea tanker to be transported to some other part. For instance, an ocean-going oil tanker would leave this country with the parts of one or more petrol carriers in sections on deck. The tanker would call at an oil port and load, say, 12,000 tons of petrol and then proceed to the part of the world from which she was to operate.

On arrival at her destination the various parts of the petrol carrier would be lifted over the side and assembled afloat in about twelve hours. After assembly, the carrier would be loaded from the parent ship and deliver the petrol at points not accessible to larger craft, sometimes many miles up shallow rivers. They were mechanically propelled and fully equipped for the work they were called upon to perform. When the army advanced and supplies of petrol were required further up country, the carrier would be dismantled whilst lying alongside the tanker and the parts lifted on board. On arrival at her next station the petrol carrier would again be assembled and the same procedure followed.

One day I noticed that a member of my staff, who also slept in the basement at St. Helen's Court, was going about his work in the office wearing only one sock. In answer to my enquiry, he said that he had been unable to find the other although he was quite sure that he left both socks together when he retired the night before. Later in the day he was wearing both socks, and he told me that it had been found in a certain place by one of the fire watchers. Finding it in that certain place meant only one thing, and that was that the sock had been carried there by a rat. Now I don't mind rats when I am awake and can see them, but the possibility of them running over my face when asleep was too much. Consequently I took my pyjamas and shaving outfit that very day to the Great Eastern Hotel in Liverpool Street and afterwards spent many sleepless nights listening to the noise of bombs and guns. But this, together with the risk of a direct hit on the hotel, was preferable to sharing sleeping quarters with rats ! The hotel, by the way, had two near misses and was badly shaken.

Looking back on those years seems like a dream. It is difficult to realise that I have walked along Bishopsgate at two o'clock in the afternoon on a weekday without seeing another soul or a wheel on the road. Sometimes I had to make my way from the Great Eastern Hotel, where I had my meals, to the office, a distance of about 500 yards, under cover of shop entrances and alleyways, as the enemy bombers flew in, hotly pursued by our few but magnificent fighters, the Hurricanes and Spitfires, in one of which Miss Curchin's young brother lost his life.

When I now take lunch at the Great Eastern Hotel and see from two to three hundred people doing the same, it seems incredible that for months, four men besides myself were the only diners in that great dining room. On one occasion our lunch was cut short owing to the hotel having to be hurriedly evacuated. Upon leaving the hotel we were not allowed to take the usual route as the cause of the evacuation was evidently in that area. The only route open to us was along Old Broad Street, which brought us out at the western end of Bishopsgate. Being curious, I looked along Bishopsgate, which was quite deserted, and saw the thing which had cut short our lunch. It was a hideous land mine about three feet in diameter suspended in mid-air by its parachute, which had caught on a trade sign projecting from the side of a building within a hundred yards of the Great Eastern Hotel. Next day it had gone, having been safely removed by those courageous men who formed what was known prosaically as the " Bomb Squad."

The building in which the flat I had rented for twenty years was situated, fortunately escaped a direct hit. It was well and truly blasted five times by bombs which fell in Regents Park. On the first occasion all windows were blown into the rooms, articles on mantlepieces, sideboard and tables were swept on to the floor and everything covered with dust. A few days later men came and fitted thick weather-proof paper where the glass had been, so on subsequent occasions there wasn't any danger from flying glass, but it always puzzled me to know where all the dirt came from. It was so thick after each blasting that the patterns of the carpets were completely obliterated.

Many unexplainable things happened during that trying time. One that comes readily to mind is perhaps worth recording. It took place when we were being pestered with V.1s. Those awful things could be heard for several minutes before they arrived overhead. I have lain in my bed night after night unable to sleep because no sooner had one landed and exploded than the next could be heard on its way.

The first batch to be sent over made a sharp dive immediately the engine cut-out, so that if the noise of the engine exhaust stopped before the V.1 reached a position overhead, you knew that your name was not on that one. Later, however, they were made to glide for some distance after the engine stopped, so that no one could be sure of being out of danger until it landed and did its destructive work. The only sound made during the gliding part of its flight was like a motor car approaching at speed on a wet road.

On the occasion of which I am now thinking, I was sitting at the table in my flat, working on some problem or other. I was facing the glassless window and every half-hour or so I could pick up the sound of V.1s coming along with monotonous regularity.

Most of them went in other directions, while a few passed overhead. Those that came my way stopped the work until I was sure that the engine was not going to cut-out and the thing glide towards me. The one which caused this particular incident to be written came my way and the engine cut-out when it was about a quarter of a mile off. This was a signal to open wide one's ears and listen for the gliding noise, which became louder and louder until I was in no doubt that it was coming straight for me !

I then heard a man in the street shout " look-out," and a moment later came the awful crash. The black-out material in my windows was blown across the room and wrapped around my head and chest, my papers were swept in all directions and as usual the place and everything in it were thickly covered with dirt.

It was a moonlight night, and after putting out the electric light, I remember standing in the middle of the room looking out of the wide open window waiting for the cloud of dust and smoke to clear in order to form some idea of where the thing had landed. Presently I heard a voice with a pronounced cockney accent say "Are you all right ? " Upon turning my head to see where the voice came from, there, standing at my side, was a little man dressed in Auxiliary Fire Service uniform. I must admit to being in a bit of a daze, but I remember answering "Yes, thanks, I'm all right."

No sooner had he disappeared than I thought " how did he get in here." Thinking that I must have left the door open I went to close it, but to my surprise found it had gone from its rightful place. The force of the explosion had been sufficient to wrench the door from its fastenings and yet, and this is the strange part of this incident, my ears were so unaffected that I could hear the question put to me quite distinctly, even though I was sitting between the window and the door when the explosion occurred. A few years after this incident I began having trouble with my ears, but none could say to what it was due.

The sad part of this story is that three people in a house on the other side of the road were killed, but with pride do I add that within a few minutes, certainly before the cloud of dust and smoke had cleared, familiar bells sounded the arrival of at least three ambulances and one fire engine.

Although living in the midst of death and destruction — on the night of 10th May 1941 over one thousand seven hundred Londoners were killed — something generally happened each day which made one forget for a while the tragedy all around. On one occasion when making my way along Bishopsgate a few hours after five hundred enemy bombers had been over London, I saw a newsvendor had chalked on his board " 500 Germans called for lunch, 250 are staying for bed and breakfast." The newspapers he wanted to sell reported that our boys had " bagged " 250 of the enemy that day. I could quote many such examples of the high spirits and ready wit of those who inhabited London during those terrible years.

Some of the incidents which occurred were not a bit funny at the time, but since the return to normal living conditions they do cause me amusement whenever I think of them. There was, for instance, the occasion when I boarded a train at Bristol wearing a pair of new shoes which were none too roomy. Not only every seat in the train, but every square foot of floor space was occupied by passengers. We were literally packed like sardines in a tin. Each compartment had four or five standing passengers, and to get along the corridor between stations was quite impossible.

I was jammed in a corner seat unable to read my book and just able to extract my cigarette case and matches from my pocket when I wanted to smoke. The night was warm, and packed as we were the compartment got uncomfortably hot. Soon my feet had swollen so much that I had to ask the man next to me to give me room to bend forward so that I could take off my shoes. Shall I ever forget the relief when this was accomplished ! It was so great and the compartment so hot and stuffy that I soon went to sleep. I had travelled throughout the previous night and had had a hard day at the docks in the interval.

The train arrived at Paddington about 4 a.m. during an air raid. After some of the passengers had got out of the train and I had free use of my arms, I tried to put on my shoes, but my feet appeared to be just about two inches too long. Feeling that if my feet were cooled down I would get them into my shoes, I left the train and began walking up and down the platform. This didn't have the desired effect, however, so I thought to take a taxi. The only thing wrong with this idea was that there wasn't a taxi to be found, and after waiting for a while to see if one would turn up, I decided to walk the two miles to my flat. So off I went, with attache-case in one hand and my shoes in the other! Soon my stockinged feet got hot and sore, and I welcomed the rain which came when I had covered about half the distance. Every now and then my attention was diverted from my poor feet by the sound of a bomb on its way down, and whilst sheltering in a shop doorway or like place, I availed myself of the opportunity to sit on the ground and take the weight off my feet.

I eventually arrived at my flat and I must confess to covering the last few yards on all fours. Once inside, I threw off my wet outer garments and fell on to the bed. I was so tired that all I had time to realise before going to sleep was how lovely it was to have my legs up and supported. I couldn't have been asleep long, however, when I woke up in a panic and gazed at my feet. The reason for my panic was that I had dreamed that my feet were getting bigger and bigger at a rate which would soon cause them to burst! After reassuring myself that my feet were not abnormally large and that it was just a dream, I went to sleep and had what I believe to be the longest unbroken sleep I have experienced.

CHAPTER XXV

LADDER CLIMBING

AFTER having lived over three score years, I can truthfully say that whilst I cannot claim to be fully satisfied, I am well pleased with what I have achieved. Many have, of course, achieved much more, and I might have done more had a better early schooling been possible. But even with a better start, I don't think I could have got more pleasure from my endeavours to do the best for myself and those dependent upon me.

I have experienced the rough as well as the smooth in life. I began my career by having to walk long distances because I hadn't the money to pay the train or tram fares, and now I use my legs only when I feel I am in need of exercise. I have worked in second-hand clothes and studied second-hand books, the books sometimes reduced in price to a few coppers because of their age and dilapidated condition. Now I can have all the new clothes and books I want.

The true value of all such things in life can only be judged by comparison, and those who have not had to go without the best cannot enjoy to the same extent the things which make life more pleasant. I am fortunate, also, in that my progress has been gradual and thus was I able to keep everything in its proper perspective. In other words, I have not under-valued anything which came my way.

Few have worked harder, firstly with their hands and afterwards with their heads. Often have I worked round the clock under conditions hardly fit for humans. My record for continuous manual work is fifty-one hours in a hot and dirty ship's engine room, with short breaks for food and rest, while my working day since beginning my apprenticeship must have averaged about fourteen hours. At the same time none have enjoyed their leisure more. I have had many friends who had no particular interest in my work, but having the capacity to put such matters completely out of my mind when together, I have derived much pleasure from their society. I have always appreciated the saying "All work and no play makes John a dull boy."

Hard work rarely causes premature death, but worry has killed many. The men and women who by their efforts have cultivated the art of doing their work without unduly worrying when things go wrong have accomplished a great deal. Those who do not worry to some extent on some occasions are so few that they are considered not quite normal. A certain degree of anxiety is necessary in order to stimulate the qualities required to overcome difficulties, but too much will have the opposite effect. The aim should be to acquire the capacity to turn one's thoughts in the direction of less perplexing matters and return to the cause of the anxiety with a mind refreshed.

The time spent writing a new edition of one of my technical books, comprising nearly one thousand pages and over three hundred drawings, averaged about three hours a day, seven days a week for three years, on top of my normal day's work. This was made possible by acquiring the habit of making good use of time spent walking, waiting for trains, during breaks for meals, and other odd times. Much of my writing and inventing was done during long train journeys in this country and abroad, which, apart from being profitable, prevented me getting bored, as do so many in such circumstances.

Fifteen minutes or so each day with a newspaper has kept me up to date, if not well informed, about events in the world outside my particular sphere, while the non-technical books which interest me most are autobiographies. It has always fascinated me to learn in a man's own words what he has done with his life.

I have experienced bitter disappointments and sometimes felt that the bottom had fallen out of my life. Two such occasions come readily to mind, the first being soon after I had completed my apprenticeship, when I missed the opportunity of a free three year course at a technical college, simply because of my eagerness to go to sea to gain experience and, incidentally, earn more money. The news I longed for but for which I did not wait, came when I was at the other side of the world and unable to return in time to take advantage of that golden opportunity. The second occasion came a few years later when I was making satisfactory progress and the future seemed bright. Then, in an instant, I met with an accident which for a time looked like bringing my engineering career to an end.

Some of my friends think I work too hard. That they are sincere in what they say and desire only that I should get the most out of my remaining years, I have not the slightest doubt. Their solicitude, bless them, is mainly prompted by the knowledge that my health is not as good as it might be, and that if I continue to work as I do now I will miss some pleasures they think are my due, and perhaps depart this world earlier than I would do if I accepted their advice.

I do not take their advice. The reason is not because I don't value their views, but because I have given the matter careful thought and having a better knowledge of my weakness, as well as my strength, I am quite convinced that by working as I do I not only get the most out of life, but will live longer. It is not right to generalise in such matters. It all depends upon the individual. Are we not told that out of the thousands of millions of people in the world there are not two exactly alike ?

Take for instance, my sight. I lost one of my eyes when twenty-four years of age and at the time was told by the doctors to avoid straining the remaining eye, which, when applied generally, would be sound advice. Since that time I have lived many years in tropical climes and must have spent on an average five hours a day reading and writing, much of it in artificial light. A foolish practice I enjoyed when out East was to watch the wonderful sunsets, sometimes until my head ached. Had my friends of that period known to what use I was putting my one eye, they would have expected me to have gone blind long ago, a fate which would perhaps have overcome many. And what is the position today ? It is, that within the last year, an able eye specialist said that my eye is perfectly healthy and that I can safely continue using it as in the past.

What is one man's meat is another man's poison is a very true saying. This applies to everything, including work. Even among the healthy, physical effort will have an adverse effect upon some while it has no such effect on others, or might even have a beneficial effect. The capacity for work does not depend solely upon physical strength. Hard mental work can have a physically stimulating effect. The man or woman with the will to work will do more and do it better than one not possessing such a desirable quality. For proof of this, look at the men who in spite of physical disabilities have by their industry and determination contributed so much to the progress of mankind. Do we need a finer example than Cecil Rhodes, who as a young man was sent to Rhodesia because it was thought that he had not long to live and that such a temperate climate would prolong his life for a few years..

What creates the will to work ? Broadly speaking it results either from the desire to keep body and soul together, or to improve one's social position. No longer is it necessary to fight, steal, or even work, to continue existing on this planet, not in our country at any rate, so that, still broadly speaking, those who do work do so either to improve their social position or for some higher motive.

There are some who have no desire to acquire more of the world's good things than they already possess, and yet keep on working. This proves, does it not, that there must be some incentive other than the improving of one's social position ? Some will say that such people love or are interested in their work, but that is only half the answer. Why do they love their work ? Is it not because of the satisfaction they get from achieving something worth while ? People who love to work, whether it be in the home, the factory or the office, invariably do good work. Are not such people inspired, and is not the real incentive a desire to serve others, or, in other words, make their full contribution to the great scheme of which our world is only a part ?

The qualities which I consider make for success are interest, common sense, curiosity and perseverance.

Interest in one's occupation is the first essential. It is not always inherent but it can be stimulated and acquired by getting to know more about the reason for and the effect of one's work.

Common sense, like interest, is not always innate, but is a quality which can be acquired. On occasions when it is noticeably lacking, it is sometimes due to inability to marshal facts, but generally it is the result of not giving sufficient thought before acting, and without full appreciation of the consequences. In other words, impetuosity is responsible for most senseless acts.

Curiosity is a natural attribute of interest, but mostly it is a quality which is developed. It is the quality which accumulates knowledge and knowledge is, of course, essential to success. Curiosity takes nothing for granted, it must know the why and wherefore of everything down to the smallest detail. All big things are made up of small things, and if the small things are not fully understood it is not possible to make a success of the big things.

Perseverance, or determination, the quality which overcomes obstacles, is very necessary to success. One who readily gives in will never experience the great thrill of achievement. There is a saying " Everything comes to those who wait." Some things may come by the exercise of patience, but for success it is true to say that everything comes to those who are determined to get what they want.

There are, of course, other aids to success. For instance, it is necessary to be able to concentrate. This will be facilitated as interest is stimulated. Memory training is another valuable aid. Reading aloud slowly and with expression helps both concentration and retention. " Blind " reading is also very helpful, particularly if a passage is not fully understood. This means reading the passage, closing the eyes and repeating it aloud over and over again until it is impressed upon the mind. If the fault lies in the writer's selection and arrangement of words, it is then easier to arrive at the meaning by analysing and re-building the passage in your own words.

Everyone has the capacity for learning. Some learn more quickly than others it is true, and they are referred to as clever. Clever ones reach their goal more quickly but do not always stay there. Those who do not have to expend much effort to acquire knowledge sometimes become over-confident, and, in engineering at any rate, are apt to make serious mistakes. Those not so gifted, providing they have other desirable qualities, will in the end be equally successful, and generally hold on to their positions because they think long and carefully before acting.

The men who can make snap decisions which always prove right are rare. Such men are born leaders. They would probably be outstanding anywhere, but in big business they must have the help of men of the plodder type who have acquired knowledge the hard way, and who in consequence are reliable and trustworthy. Those who feel that they have not been specially endowed with brain, should not, therefore, be discouraged.

Because I have written books which have become world famous in shipping circles, and in recent years have been able to find solutions to age-old problems, many think I am clever, while those who are envious, think I am lucky. Both views are quite wrong. Considering the time I have spent acquiring what little I now know, and how difficult it has been, and is still, to improve my knowledge, I don't know which view I dislike most. It is not complimentary to say that success is due to having a greater weight of grey matter than others who have been less successful, when it is the result of hard work and determination to get on.

When I began my engineering apprenticeship and saw huge engines, the like of which I had never dreamed, hundreds of noisy wheels revolving and levers oscillating for reasons quite beyond my comprehension, and cranes lifting and conveying without apparent effort, lumps of iron weighing, what seemed to me, hundreds of tons, I felt that it would be quite impossible for me to learn about such things. This impression was forcibly confirmed when a fellow apprentice showed me his book on mathematics, and painfully when I first attempted to use a hammer and chisel.

This feeling of absolute impotence lasted until I plucked up courage to put questions to the men whom I judged would remember the day when they knew no more than I did then and give me truthful answers. Thus the little interest I had in the things around me caused me to ask questions, and the answers I got stimulated that interest. After a time I realised that all big things were made up of little things, and that it was the little things and not the big things about which I had to learn first. This didn't seem such a formidable task to my immature mind, and the desire to learn rapidly grew.

During the years which followed, learning became less difficult, and by the time I reached the end of my apprenticeship I thought I knew all there was to know about engineering. My first voyage to sea as a junior engineer, however, quickly disillusioned me, and ever since the realisation of how little I know and how much more there is still to learn has never left me.

The tendency today is towards more theory. This is all to the good so long as it is not obtained at the expense of practice. For success in shipping the two must go hand in hand. It is not sufficient to know how a job should be done. To be able to do it is very important. It would be easy to quote scores of examples where lack of practical knowledge would result in a very serious situation. Theory may prevent undesirable things happening, but only practice can minimise the adverse effect when they do happen. For instance, theory may prevent a ship running aground but only practice will re-float her.

One of the secrets of success in almost every field of human activity is to learn by doing things rather than by watching how things are done. You can only learn about manual work by working manually, and if an engineering profession is chosen, sweat, dirt and bruised and blistered hands are things that must be endured philosophically. To be a real leader of men one must have their respect, and this is more likely to be achieved if in addition to being able to do work which they cannot do, you can do the men's work as well as they can do it themselves.

A view prevalent among young men today is that there are not nearly so many opportunities for advancement as there were before all the things we now see around us were discovered. They feel that the two previous generations have done all there is to do in pioneering and the only thing left for them is work of a hum-drum routine character. Nothing is further from the truth. The fact is that there are far more opportunities today for concentrated effort than ever before, and in a hundred years from now there will be many more opportunities than there are at the present time.

Every new discovery opens up scores of avenues which require to be developed and perfected. Each new discovery can be likened to a sapling. At first there is the trunk, then when it has taken root branches begin to shoot out from the trunk. Later, smaller branches shoot out from the main branches, and so on.

Take any of the great basic discoveries of the past century in the engineering profession alone, the steam engine, the electric motor, wireless waves, to mention only a few, and you will find that while the discovery of each offered one opportunity, the development of each multiplied the number of opportunities a great many times.

Yes, there is still much to be done before we can claim to make the best use of the wonderful things this world contains. Not only have many forces yet to be discovered, but none of the forces so far discovered has been completely developed. We still use fuel very wastefully ; the steam engine which has been with us for over a hundred years still makes good use of less than one-half of the fuel it consumes. Accidents still happen and lives are lost by fatigue and failure of mechanical devices, one can't travel by land, sea or air without being subjected to either noise or vibration, both of which have a more harmful effect upon the health of people than is generally realised.

Even in this supposedly enlightened age we cannot build a draught-proof house nor prevent loss of life and property by fire. Look at the steel which corrodes away each year, the present estimate is 40 million tons, despite the enormous sums of money and manual effort expended in producing and applying paint. What about the present method of lighting the streets of our towns at night ? Can such a method which gives a small circle of light here and there at enormous cost be called satisfactory ? There is no end to the list. I could go on and on, but these few may be sufficient to convince those young people that we are a very long way from reaching the state of perfection which the Lord who makes all things possible intended.

I have no regrets that I was put to engineering, although there have been times when I thought the work too hard and far from congenial. All my working life I have had a desire to improve the design and capacity of machines and structures, but the opportunity didn't come my way for a long time because the acquisition of specialised knowledge had to be secondary to earning a living. Nevertheless, I have on a few occasions given the former priority by accepting lower paid positions when I felt I could gain further knowledge without imperilling my living.

The opportunity for which I have prepared myself has now come and I am revelling in my endeavours to solve age-old problems. The work is particularly gratifying, as the ultimate effect of any success is either to raise the standard of living by reducing the cost to produce or transport the things our present civilisation requires, or to eliminate the grief which results from violent death or serious injury in industry.

EPILOGUE

THE Almighty has indeed been good to me. From this you will rightly assume that I believe in the existence of a Power far greater than anything on earth. I cannot conceive that we humans, with such wonderful faculties and delicate emotions, our world of wealth and beauty and universe so vast and complex, could have come by chance. No one who has studied the laws of nature, so perfect and so enduring, or even taken the trouble to learn a little about the things which are generally taken for granted, could think otherwise.

I am convinced that this world on which we live is only a part, and perhaps a very small part, of a vast scheme, the purpose of which, even if explained, we could not understand because we do not yet have the mental capacity to understand. It would be like teaching a five year old child the calculus. The time will surely come, however, when we shall be able to understand all that is now so perplexing, and those who have endeavoured to make use of the qualities which God has given to develop the resources of the world for the good of all, and who by thoughtfulness for others have tried to make this world a better place, will ultimately have reason to be well pleased that they did so.

Even the most knowledgable know so little about the things which really matter that in ignorance some not only tolerate, but actually believe, the outpourings of self-styled demi-gods that spring up from time to time and disturb the peace of the world. They may succeed in altering the trend of things on earth for a time, but the fact that they ever existed is soon forgotten, while every natural law, not one of which they are capable of altering in the smallest degree, will continue to function to the end of all things on earth as they have from the beginning, now so far remote that it is doubtful if it will ever be known on earth when it took place.

These supposedly supermen, and many others whose names do not make newspaper headlines but who brag and boast of their power, evidently do not make themselves aware of the wonders all around. If they did they would surely realise that whilst some progress has been made in developing the world's resources, even to the extent of splitting the atom, man is only at the beginning of his endeavours, and the whole of mankind's efforts to date can be likened to something less than a drop of water in the ocean.

Puny man prides himself upon producing power to drive ships, trains, airplanes and weapons of war, but there is more power released from a flash of lightning than is produced by mechanical means in years.

When speaking of atom bombs we think we know something about bombardments, but what was the destruction of Hiroshima compared with what has been achieved outside this world. For instance, a meteorite calculated to weigh a million tons lies buried in Arizona, while another which landed on the West coast of Africa made a crater six miles in diameter and over a thousand feet deep. The impact must have been terrific, but it is doubtful if it put the world off its course the merest fraction or for an instant of time.

As many of these demi-gods as there are microbes in the earth's soil, and there are more in a handful than there are people in the world, would have been powerless to alter the course of such projectiles in the least degree.

Man thinks he dominates everything on the surface of this planet. Nothing would be further from the fact. Take, for instance, air, the presence of which is almost too obvious to be noticed, what could he do to produce it and where would he be without it ?

Without the atmosphere there would be no animal or vegetable life, no wind or rain. The heat by day would be intense and the cold by night unbearable. Nothing would burn, therefore it would not be possible to produce warmth or power for driving ships, trains, factories or any other power-operated contrivance. At night there would be no light but what came from the heavens. No sounds would be heard because all sound is transmitted by vibrating air waves.

Even if man could exist without air he couldn't achieve any-thing. Life would be possible without any of the things made or produced by man, but if he were denied any one of nature's gifts he would soon become extinct.

Many other illustrations proving how feeble are man's efforts when compared with nature could be given. This is not surprising considering that the human race is quite a late comer to the world. None know for certain how long life on this world has existed, but available evidence suggests, if it does not prove, that life existed 300 million years ago. If, therefore, life on the earth were time-filmed and the film run continuously for twelve hours, the earliest known ape man would not appear until about the last minute.

I am of the opinion, therefore, that man is only starting the great task for which he was put upon the earth, namely, the development of the natural resources that have taken many millions of years to provide. In other words, the Creator has provided the tools and it is up to man to make good use of them so that this world of ours will become a perfect part of the great scheme which He is evolving for the good of all.

Men of all colours and creeds, as well as all living things, have their part to play. Some of the things about us seem purposeless, but that is only because our knowledge is so very limited. Just as people of a hundred years ago thought as of no good purpose some of the things which we are using today with advantage, so will the people of a million, thousand, or even a hundred years from now think of many things for which we have no use. With the development of the earth's natural resources will come a better understanding among the people of the earth and ultimately there will be heaven on earth, in accordance with the teachings of Jesus Christ.